Belonging

Overcoming rejection and finding
the freedom of acceptance

Nancy and Ron Rockey
with Kay Kuzma

a sycamore tree book
from
Pacific Press® Publishing Association
Nampa, Idaho
Oshawa, Ontario, Canada
www.pacificpress.com

Designed by Michelle Petz
Cover photos represent six generations from the Rockey
photo album.

Copyright © 1998 by
Pacific Press® Publishing Association
Printed in the United States of America
All Rights Reserved

Additional copies of this book may be purchased at
http://www.adventistbookcenter.com

Cataloging-in-Publication Library of Congress Data
Rockey, Nancy, 1943-
    Belonging : overcoming rejection and finding freedom of
acceptance / Nancy and Ron Rockey, with Kay Kuzma.
        p. cm.
    ISBN 0-8163-1702-X (pbk.)
    1. Adult child abuse victims—Religious life. 2. Christian
life.
I. Rockey, Ron, 1941-   . II. Kuzma, Kay. III.Title.
BV 4596.A25R63 1999
261.8'3273—dc21   99-24436
                                                              CIP

01 02 03 • 5 4 3

About the Authors

Ron Rockey, Ph.D. and Nancy Rockey, Ph.D.

Internationally recognized seminar leaders and counseling psychologists, Drs. Ron and Nancy Rockey are one of the foremost Christian couples working in the area of recovery.

Inspired by their own personal healing and growth, and thousands of testimonies of people they have helped throughout their twenty-five years of team ministry, they have developed an incredibly successful recovery plan based on the Bible and Inspiration.

Over thirty years of marriage, the parenting of two daughters, and extensive graduate work have provided a testing and proving ground for the effective tools they recommend for personal and relational growth.

Their graduate studies have prepared them as Marriage and Family Therapists (M.Ed.) and Counseling Psychologists (Ph.D.). In addition to being state licensed counselors, Ron is also a minister and Nancy a registered nurse.

They have taught and lectured internationally, have appeared on national television talk shows, and co-hosted a live daily radio talk program.

Together they have shared their knowledge and experience with interdenominational church groups and conferences. They currently are the family health ministry team for the television ministry *Faith for Today*.

"Our conviction is that much pain and sorrow can be alleviated through knowledge and understanding. We have dedicated our lives to teaching and providing tools for a rapid recovery. To us, there is no greater joy than to see the eyes of understanding opened, hurting changed into healing, and conflict transformed into compatibility." (Ron and Nancy Rockey)

Kay Kuzma, Ed.D.

Dr. Kay Kuzma, child development and family life specialist, is president of Family Matters and host of the syndicated daily radio program *Got a Minute for Your Family?* She publishes *Family Times*, a newspaper for parents, and is the author of more than a dozen books, including *Easy Obedience* and *Creating Love*. In addition, she is a popular speaker and seminar leader with a master's degree in child development from Michigan State University and a doctorate in early childhood education from UCLA. She and her husband, Jan, live in Tennessee and have three grown children.

In the process of recovery

one cannot hope to alter history.

God, who is omniscient and controls the

past, present, and future,

however,

can so alter the present

that the pain is removed from the past.

Nancy Rockey

Contents

Acknowledgments

To our family who created us and gave us all of the experiences about which we write. For the good and not so good. The mosaic of our lives has been made beautiful by your love, even when we didn't feel its warmth.

To our children, our precious miracle girls, who tolerated us in our weakness and ignorance and have grown up to be loving and kind. We love you.

To those balcony people who cheered us on in spite of our faults and foibles and to those who have taught and mentored us along the way. We thank you.

Dedication

With love and gratitude this book is dedicated
to the memory of our friend and mentor,
Harry Anderson
He brought Christ to us through his inspired art
and through his Christlike character.
"It's all in the eye; in how you observe
what you can see," he said.
"You must train the eye to see all that there is;
all of the colors, bold AND subtle,
all of the delicate hues which combine
to make the object what it is;
that's what a true artist does.
It's not so much in the hand, as it is in training the hand
to create what the eye observes."
We agree, Harry.
A true artist has a keen eye,
and you had the sharpest of all!
For in our weakness, you saw strength; in our sorrow,
you saw a brighter day; in our raw inexperience,
you saw polished wisdom; in our youthful enthusiasm,
you saw success; in our bold aggressiveness,
you saw courage; in our defeats, you saw the rough edges
being polished; in our gray depression,
you saw needed introspection; and in our brokenness,
you saw a teachable spirit emerging.
And in your "Father Heart,"
we found God's acceptance, compassion,
and unconditional, expectant love.
The Master Artist had used you to create
on the canvass of our lives a portrait of God,
which will bless us until we see His face
and your dear face once again.

Introduction

Ron's Story
I've been in the darkness of the dungeon,
A 4 x 6 x 6 cold damp box;
Naked and alone—very alone;
In solitary confinement behind thick cement walls
And miles of barbed wire at the state penitentiary.
I understand the torture of prejudice
And the brutality of power.

Days blurred into unending nights;
Hope faltered and died.
Release from the hole seemed impossible.

I desperately wanted out.
But someone else had the key.
I'd been stripped of my dignity,
Naked and shamed.

My strength was ebbing from poor nutrition;
My muscles flaccid with disuse.

I curled myself into a fetal position,
Yearning to return to the safety of the womb.

My thoughts condemned me.
My selfhood was gone,
And although I existed—my spirit was dead!

I've been out in the sunlight married to the woman I adore,
My daughters laughing and playing beside me.
I've fulfilled my dream of finishing graduate studies
And practicing my chosen profession,

But all the while feeling more desperate
than I did in the hole.

I've been in the spider's web.

I found the route of escape,
Both from the cement and barbed-wire prison,
And from the prison of my mind.

This book is about escape.
It's about the journey to emotional freedom.
It's about cutting the sticky strands of the web,
And being free.

Nancy's Story
I also know the torture of confinement,
but not behind cold stone walls or barbed wire.
Caged in flesh and bone, I silently feared
that being who I really was would get me
ridiculed, ignored, unapproved or rejected.

Curled on the sofa in my childhood home,
I sucked my thumb while I wished away a painful secret,
and made believe that all was well.
And as I sat, my body built unattractive walls
designed to keep intruders out,
because the safety of my home
had been violated by two men in my neighborhood.

I knew nothing of perceptions, so in my web
I saw my dad as rigid, unyielding with me,
and yet I laughed and played with him
and brought home other kids to do the same.
Admiring his wit, wisdom, and talent, I conformed
to hear the words he could not say.

Why couldn't I please him?

My soft and tender mother stroked my hair and my ears
with her velvet hands and endeavored to interpret
and convince me of Daddy's love.
But paralyzing fear colored my view of reality and truth;
so we both felt rejected by the other.
What he needed, he could not give.
I wish I'd understood then
that deeds he did and gifts he gave
replaced his words unsaid
and that his disappointment shown
was his praise, disguised.

But this was not to be
until I discovered that knowledge is the key
and courage opens the door.

This book is about escape from prisons.
It's about the journey to emotional freedom.
It's about cutting the sticky strands of the web,

And being free.

*"Oh, Lord, Shine Your light and
reveal to us our inner selves.
Free us from chains which bind us
to immaturity and childishness.
Prepare our hearts for wholeness
and fullness in Your Spirit."*

David A. Seamands

CHAPTER 1

Trapped in the Spider's Web

"I, the Lord, have called you . . .
To open eyes that are blind,
to free captives from prison and
to release from the dungeon
those who sit in darkness."
Isaiah 42:6, 7, NIV

We have lived imprisoned by the past and have found the escape route. We have felt the chains of rejection; they have cut deep into the flesh of our souls, and now we enjoy the freedom of feeling, accepted for who we are. What we share with you is what we have learned through the rocky road we have traveled during the last half century. This isn't just book knowledge. It's gut knowledge too. It's the story of Holy Spirit insight that our wonderful Father in heaven has revealed to us; the message of His love and of the conflict between good and evil in which we found ourselves trapped.

(Ron) Although Nancy's entrapment was internal while living in a cozy, warm home, mine was cold and outwardly abusive, leading to the most cruel confinement anyone can experience—a 4 x 6 x 6 isolation chamber within a southern prison.

Feelings of rejection had surfaced while I was still in the crib and intensified throughout childhood. The anger that normally results from rejection turned into rebellion that manifested itself in various pranks, which became more cruel with the years. Shortly after my father's death, I was sent by a judge into the navy rather than prison. I was seventeen, and the need to numb my pain, as I had been doing in civilian life, escalated with each day. It required a lot of alcohol to exist only sober enough to do my job, and the navy pay was never sufficient to meet the needs that my emotional deficit demanded.

Once discharged, I did whatever petty thievery I needed to do in order to stay anesthetized. One scheme led to another, one arrest led to others, and I found myself behind bars, shuffled from prison to prison until I finally hit Tennessee's "big house."

It was in a smaller prison that I got severely sunburned while working in the Tennessee sun. Motor oil, the guard's answer to ward off a sunburn, only served to "cook" my skin so that my body was a swollen and blistered balloon. Begging for an indoor pass from the infirmary only angered my guard who said, "Well, Boy, you'll get your indoor pass all right. Follow me!"

Stripped of clothing, I was shoved in "the hole" and fed bread and water for several weeks. There I was in total isolation, in a dank and smelly cave with nothing to do but contemplate my life; endure the acute physical pain; sense the icy rejection of family, friends, and society; and feel the ever-increasing internal rage burning within me.

Have you ever felt you were trapped in a web of circumstances and regardless of what you did, you just couldn't escape? Perhaps you feel that way now.

Maybe you feel alone even though people are all around you. Everyone else seems to be part of the group, but you feel isolated—rejected by them all. Do you wonder how others can be so lighthearted, while your own heart is so heavy?

Maybe you have fits of anger that surprise you. Or you can't seem to control sudden outbursts with your children, even though you know better, and you have promised yourself—and them—you'll never do it again.

At times do you feel like a child? You just don't seem to have the emotions or the capabilities of a mature adult. You act impulsively and irresponsibly.

Do you find yourself attracted to the same type of life partners who end up beating you up emotionally or physically? Why are you always the rejected victim?

Maybe you find yourself frequently disappointed in your relationship with God—you just can't seem to connect. It feels as though He doesn't want you either.

Is your life a series of disasters? Are you your own worst enemy—sabotaging your own success and distancing yourself from others by something you've said or done?

Why does everyone else seem so organized and in control of their lives, and you're like a boat without a rudder, pushed this way and that by every breeze that blows? You seem to get nowhere because you spend all your energy dancing to someone else's tune just to be accepted.

Do you perform for acceptance, playing to the crowd rather than being the real you? Will you do almost anything to be loved?

It could be reoccurring feelings of "I'm never good enough" that drive you to either become a workaholic for approval from the boss or to give up from a defeated attitude of "Why try? Nobody cares anyway."

Maybe you dread Mother's Day or Father's Day. You feel guilty that you don't want to send a card or you spend all your time looking for a card that doesn't have the word *love* in it because you didn't feel their love as a child.

Do you feel as if life has dealt you a losing hand—that when beauty, talent, and brains were distributed, you didn't get your fair share?

Do you sometimes vision sexual encounters with partners not your own? Or maybe you're attracted to pornography, peep shows, prostitution or massage parlors, as though one more sexual encounter would fill the empty place in your heart with acceptance.

Why is it that you can't seem to keep friends, or when a friendship progresses to a certain point, you pull away, or they quit calling? Does it feel as if you are always being rejected?

Do you wish you could sometimes just go to sleep and never wake up?

If any of these things sound familiar, we have good news for you: You don't have to be a fly entangled in a web, waiting for the spider to strike. You don't have to fear his poisonous venom. You *can* have your blind eyes opened to understand the reasons behind your behavior. You *can* escape from the prison of your mind and the fear of rejection. You *can* be released from the dungeon of darkness and experience the light of liberty. (See Isa. 42:7.) *You can escape the spider's web.*

The answer is in understanding the driving force behind your actions. You can't escape personal responsibility by blaming others or circumstances, and actually assigning blame is a counterproductive activity. The only way to get out of the trap is to acknowledge the real and insidious nature of the struggle you are experiencing.

The truth is that a force you never before may have identified is driving your thoughts and feelings of rejection, controlling your behaviors, and stealing the abundant life Christ wants you to experience. Jesus says, "The thief (Satan) does not come except to steal, and to kill, and to destroy. I have come that they may have life, and that they may have it more abundantly" (John 10:10, NKJV).

Some may question the existence of Satan and his angels, but it is hardly sensible to believe in God and His Word and not believe what He teaches about the reality of Satan, His enemy. C. S. Lewis in his preface to the allegory, *Screwtape Letters*, states, "There are two equal and opposite errors into which our race can fall about the devils. One is to disbelieve in their existence. The other is to believe, and to feel an excessive and unhealthy interest in them" (15). Satan is the father of lies, and he has told you a whopper—that you are of no worth or value. He wants you to feel the same stab of rejection he feels from God, as a result of his choice to reject God. If you can feel rejected, you'll end up just like him—hopeless.

God doesn't play games. But Satan's game is that the one with the most converts wins. Like in a giant chess battle, Satan is out for as many checkmates as he can get. Although he knows he has already lost to the God of the universe, he doesn't want to go down alone. You are his pawn. Misery loves company. The end is near. His fury is increased. He walks around like a roaring lion seeking whom he can destroy. And so he configures circumstances so as to resurface and exaggerate your early childhood pain.

Satan's plan is, if possible, to destroy you and your children. For in destroying you, he will affect your children, and theirs—unto the third and fourth generation and on and on—unless you take the personal responsibility necessary to stop the cycle and seek recovery. You must be willing to say "The pain of rejection stops here with me. I will no longer be the pawn in the devil's game of chess; I will no longer carry the devil's garbage." If you don't make this a lifetime commitment, you will agree to allow Satan to pass on your garbage and his, in ever-increasing weight and stench, to your children and grandchildren.

The damage Satan does to children creates a paralysis of the senses. As adults, we are then deaf to warnings or reproofs, and reformation of the life is nearly impossible.

The lie

Let us explain to you the insidious nature of Satan's methods to lead humanity astray. It all began in the Garden of Eden when Eve wandered away from her husband's side. Granted, she was beguiled by an attractive talking serpent; in short, she was tempted. But she seemed to be knowledgeable regarding God's law about the tree of the knowledge of good and evil. In fact, she added to God's words saying that the fruit of the tree should not even be touched. Even so, Satan managed to convince Eve that God was just attempting to keep from them a knowledge He possessed and that if she ate of the tree, she would be like God who knows good from evil.

Up to that point, Adam and Eve had only eaten from the tree of life and other life-giving trees in the garden, so what she and Adam had known only pertained to life.

After partaking of the forbidden tree's fruit, however, Adam and Eve were not only ashamed, but they began immediately to know of death. Their guilt, which was new to them at that moment, led them to shame, which led them to hide from God and attempt to cover their guilt and shame with fig leaves. This was the beginning of their dying process.

The choice was given by a loving God who did not want Adam and Eve and the generations to follow (which He had given them procreation ability to create) to be automatons but compliant partners and intimate friends of God. Unfortunately, sin produced in Adam and Eve a disease (lack of ease) with which succeeding generations have had to either fight or resign themselves to endure.

At the core of every human being existing since Adam and Eve, and in those alive today, there is a lie implanted by God's enemy. It became a part of Adam and Eve when they sinned, and they proved it by hiding from God and by attempting to cover themselves with leaves. *This lie states that you have no worth and value.* As you look internally at your thoughts and feelings (character) and outwardly at your behaviors, you are convinced that the lie is truth. The cosmetic and fashion industries of today make their fortunes by those of us who feel that we must cover or camouflage what we are convinced is truth—our worthlessness.

The lie comes to us in the direct line from Adam and Eve and has intensified in its power with each succeeding generation. We have passed that lie from grandparent to parent to child ever since time began, and by this generation have become quite sophisticated in the ways we cover up. Our fig leaves have become our clothes, our make-up, our masks of falsehood we wear for the world to see. We observe our parents, relatives, and friends in childhood and learn well how to perpetuate the lie.

So the lie comes to us first by *inheritance.* Additionally, the lie comes to us from our *environment.* The families, churches, and communities in which we were raised have, in most cases, assisted us to feel that we have little or no worth and value because our long list of needs were unmet or ignored. When children do not get their basic needs met (see chapter 8), then they interpret that they are not worthy of the attention and caring they need. Neglect acts as an exclamation point behind the lie at our core, which we inherited from preceding generations, and we become even more convinced that we are unloved and unlovable. Our parents did not purposefully choose to not meet our needs, but they were simply the product of their previous generation, and their needs went unmet also.

Third, the lie is accentuated by the *experiences* of life that have brought specific damages to us, such as rejection, sexual abuse, emotional and/or physical abuse. In any of these damages, children take the responsibility because of the internal lie they carry and because children automatically feel responsible for whatever goes wrong in their world.

If the parents or others, who were supposed to be nurturing to the children, also dump guilt on them by blaming them either by actual accusation or inference, the children are doomed to carry this load of guilt and shame until somehow they are hopefully interrupted by truth.

As we age, it becomes increasingly more difficult to contradict what we have come to believe about ourselves, thus harder to change the negative and defeating course of our lives. In actuality, we fear any information which contradicts what we have come to believe about ourselves. We've become convinced that we are inferior, weak, worthless, evil, and shameful, and we resist attempts to change these beliefs. When you consider that our belief system is mostly set in place by the age of eight, you can realize that most of us spend our lives living a lie. We develop words to cover it and share them with others by either boasting of our greatness or boasting of our worthlessness. Either end of the pendulum swing—the superiority complex or the inferiority complex—will tick the same clock. Think about how many half or partial truths we tell in an effort to cover up the feelings we have about ourselves. Think about it, What are some of the favorite partial truths you use?

The lies we tell to cover the lie at our core forces us into behaviors we feel are imperative to mask the lie. We become codependent in our relationships, because we are convinced we cannot make it on our own without someone to tell us what to do and how to do it or to applaud our every attempt at goodness. We become addicted to the numbing substances of alcohol, drugs, TV, sex, shopping, work, religion, or even sleep. We live in houses, wear clothes, and drive cars far beyond our incomes, which makes it necessary to work harder to purchase all the cover-ups. We paint our faces, shorten our noses, color our hair, wear false fingernails, become do-gooders, eat too much, starve ourselves, and paste on smiles so that the world will think we have it all together!

One of the greatest fears of humankind is that we will somehow come to a knowledge of our true selves. What would happen, we wonder, if we would come to realize that we really are loving or creative or talented in some way? That knowledge would require us to make changes in our behaviors and lifestyles, and change is frightening. Any knowledge that would move us from our conscious position of worthlessness is translated by us as a falsehood, thus dangerous, and most will bristle at the thought of it. We resist personal growth in any manner, because it brings other fears with it. What would happen if we discovered in the process of growth that we are really weak or inadequate, which we already know at the core of our being? What affect would this have on us, and how could we change that? We sacrifice our personal happiness in activities, goals, dreams, accomplishments, and, most frighteningly, in intimate relationships, all to protect a lie. What a merry-go-round of nonsense and pain we live on, protecting an untruth given to us by the father of lies! We feel unworthy of giving up the pain we carry from childhood injustices, and we fear any knowledge that might cause us to despise ourselves as it uncovers that weakness and worthlessness that we feel.

We have wondered if the resistance to growth and character development we see in many might be connected to the fact that Eve's investigation of the tree of the knowledge of good and evil brought about her demise, and from her, succeeding generations of ever-increasing sinfulness leading to eternal loss. If that could be the case, we have somehow turned things topsy-turvy. It was not eating from the tree of life that brought about her destruction. Had she continued to enjoy it, we would not be fighting the battles we fight today. The tree of life is found in the Word, and when we ingest its truths into our souls, it gives us light and life! Deuteronomy 5:29 (NIV) pleads: "Oh that their hearts would be inclined to fear Me [adore Me with tender feeling] and keep all my commands always, so that it might go well with them and their children forever." Verse 33 continues: "Walk in all the way that the Lord your God has commanded you, so that you may live and prosper and prolong your days in the land that you will possess."

What we have not realized before is that what happened to us in childhood has become the filter through which all other life experiences have passed. The unresolved pain we carry today colors today's experiences, thus our thoughts and feelings about them and our behaviors result from them. Often these are as destructive to us as it was for Eve to partake of the forbidden fruit. What a sad thing it is that we have been blessed with the solution all along but have not realized that recovery from these defeating thoughts and feelings was possible. We have interpreted falsely that we had to endure the hurt, gritting our teeth and bearing it until Jesus comes. When Jesus tells us that we can come to Him, laden with heavy burdens and exhausted from the laborious task of carrying the ever increasing load, He is speaking of the dumpster full of the pain Satan wants us to carry, exhausting us so much that we will be discouraged, feel hopeless, and give up. The Manual of Life tells us how to give up the load, but we have been blinded by evil forces so we will misinterpret and misunderstand the method. When we choose to follow God's plan, we choose to eat of the tree that inevitably leads to eternal life.

The truth

God created you, died to redeem you, and has a plan of salvation for you. You are rightfully an important part of His royal family—if you choose to be. You can escape from Satan's web of deceit if you choose. *But choice requires making a decision*—a rational decision. Satan knows this and, therefore, his master plot is to destroy the rational decision-making abilities of God's children. Satan has devised a subtle scheme to do this through the pain you have suffered in your past. Each painful experience leaves you feeling rejected in some way. Like a killer virus introduced into a computer system, damage scrambles your decision-making capability. It confuses your feelings, causing them to control your thoughts and actions. The result is that you end up doing what you don't want to do, controlled by a compelling power within that you don't understand, thus making the choice of accepting Christ difficult.

To further paralyze his prey, Satan knows if he can keep the filing cabinet of your mind (the subconscious) filled with destructive feelings of rejection from the emotionally charged painful memories of needs unmet and past injustices done, he can force you to see every current circumstance through the distorted glasses of rejection. You will search everywhere for evidence to corroborate his original lie that for you, acceptance is unattainable.

In the scientific realm, the law of displacement states that no two things can occupy the same space at the same time. It is also true that the mind cannot be filled with emotionally-charged memories of pain and injustice, while at the same time be filled with the overflowing love of God.

Satan's plan to defeat humanity is one of self-destruction, starting with children. Randall Tarry, co-founder of Operation Rescue, was quoted in the October 21, 1991, issue of *Time* magazine as saying, "I believe there is a devil, and here's Satan's agenda. First, he doesn't want anyone having kids. Secondly, if they do conceive, he wants them killed. If they're not killed through abortion, he wants them neglected or abused, physically, emotionally, sexually. . . .

"One way or another, the legions of hell want to destroy children because children become the future adults and leaders.

"If they can warp and wound a child, he or she becomes a warped or wounded adult who passes on this affliction to the next generation."

While still in the womb the mother's feelings of rejection due to her past and current experiences are transferred to the baby who then absorbs these emotions as his or her own. A young child absorbs information from the outside world through their emotions, because the logical brain is still in the early developmental stages. Satan's insidious plan is to damage a child before the brain is mature enough to be able to add the logic stored in the cerebral cortex to the emotion felt at the moment, which is necessary for mature decision making. This makes children incredibly vulnerable to their present circumstances. Everything they experience, whether actual or perceived, becomes a part of their conscious or sub-conscious emotional memory bank.

It is during these character-forming years that Satan attempts to sting children with His poisonous venom and emotionally paralyze them for life by causing them to suffer from unmet needs, from sexual, emotional, or physical abuse, all of which create feelings of rejection within the child.

Early childhood is a vulnerable time for children. Before children have accepted Christ as their personal Savior and are thus under the protective covering of grace, they are the lawful prey of Satan. Before they have experienced the cleansing power of the blood of Jesus, the evil angels make every effort to gain access to them. Although children are vulnerable, they are not, however, defenseless—if they have praying parents. The protective power of their parents' faithful and untiring prayers can break the hold of the enemy. When Christ's name is called upon, the powers of darkness must retreat. But if Satan has control of parents because of the damages done to them in childhood, their children almost always end up being damaged too.

Satan first did his number on Adam and Eve in the Garden of Eden, causing guilt, disappointment, shame, and fear. Even though God had not rejected them, they felt so rejected by Him that they hid in the bushes. Bearing their own psychological pain, Adam and Eve parented their children, one of whom murdered his brother. And down through the generations the sins of the fathers and mothers have affected their children.

It's almost as if Satan is sitting back with his arms folded and his feet up on his desk saying, "I don't have to do anything more. Watch them self-destruct." Hurting human beings will do themselves in and in the process they will damage the people around them. He has thrown his rock into the lake of humanity and is watching with glee the ever widening ripples.

It is important to understand that it is not even necessary for an act to be committed to negatively influence or damage someone else. Each person is surrounded with an atmosphere, invisible to the naked eye. It is an aura that is made up of your thoughts and feelings—your character. It is your character, that secret part of you known only to God and yourself, that provides the impetus for your behaviors. This atmosphere either blesses or poisons everyone with whom you come in contact. Without so much as uttering a word that might express what you think or feel, you still affect those around you out of the context of your thinking and feeling. A person's atmosphere may be charged with the life-giving power of faith, courage, hope, and love. Or it may be heavy and chilly with the gloom of discontent and selfishness or poisonous with the deadly taint of cherished sin. Every person with whom you come in contact is consciously or unconsciously affected by the atmosphere surrounding you.

When you are in the company of one whose thoughts are for the most part centered upon selfish anger, greed, or lust, you will feel unsafe, uncomfortable, and will choose to remove yourself to a protected place. Even young children who may lack the words to express their feelings of fear can sense this with some adults and will refuse to go near or be held by them. That unsafe atmosphere is the poison that creates a damage even without a word spoken or an action taken.

Satan's tangled web of sins and the resulting pain passed down from generation to generation can be overpowering, unless you understand the source of your driven behaviors, acknowledge the damage done to you, take responsibility for your actions, and learn to use the weapons God has made available for His children to be victorious.

We have discovered that most people with a teachable spirit who are given the knowledge and the tools can, through the power of God, work through their own issues and break the cycle of damage. The unfortunate fact is that most people don't seek recovery before they reach thirty or forty years of age. Therefore, healing comes after their children's vulnerable years, so the damage has already been inflicted on the next generation. The good news is that if you as parents are willing to look in the mirror of God's Word to see your own weaknesses and dysfunctional tendencies and are willing to uncover the origin of your behaviors in order to discover the way out, *your children are positively affected by the character changes they observe in you, their parents, regardless of age or physical distance.*

Because this is a warfare between Christ and Satan, no human being is excluded. Sin has a magnetic pull on our vulnerable minds. Too often when persons desire to return to God, they can find themselves entangled in such a network of Satan, like a fly in a spider's web, that it seems a hopeless task to them, and they give up, rather than doing the work necessary for emotional and spiritual recovery. (See chapter 11.)

Ringing in our ears are the words of Julie, who was desperately seeking healing for the results of the abuse she had suffered in childhood: "I have always longed for a relationship with God. And I keep trying. I read my Bible, but I don't get anything from it. I pray, but it feels like they are empty words that I'm hollering out into the wind. Why is it everybody else can find God and I can't? I finally decided that it must be me. I must have done something to alienate God from me forever." This is the lie that Satan wants us to believe.

The concept of Satan, as the black widow spider weaving his web to catch and destroy us, came to me (Nancy) as a direct answer to prayer. I had never read the above passage until after this experience.

It was a frigid cold Dakota morning, the kind of morning that begs one to linger in a warm bed or to bake homemade bread and cut up vegetables for a steaming bowl of hearty stew. But I had an appointment at the office. As I started the Saab and headed downtown, I prayed, "Lord, this is a new client. I don't know who she is. And this morning I don't really care. Will you make me care? Please spark my uncaring attitude with love for Your hurting child. You'll have to help me welcome this woman with your loving hospitality."

As I walked into the office complex, I was tempted to be annoyed at the cigarette smoke pouring out from the AA meeting room down the hall. I chose instead to be thankful for fragrant spray and spicy potpourri that I kept in my own counseling office. I selected two pretty china mugs and put water in the kettle to boil. Hot herb tea on a frigid morning would spell welcome.

All too soon she sat in the counseling room, her hands warming around a mug of tea. We began with my usual prayer for God's presence and wisdom, and then I asked, "What exactly brings you to the office this morning, and how can I help?"

Clutching my own tea cup, I sat back to listen to her story. But there was none. For ten minutes she rattled on incoherently. Sentences ran into fragmented sentences. Phrases made no sense; they were disconnected. I tried to pick up a theme to her speaking but couldn't find one. Perhaps her anxiety of coming to a counselor was causing this confusion and would soon dissipate. But the more she talked, the more frustrated I became. I said to myself, "Nancy, you are in way over your head this time. This one is out of touch with reality. Nothing makes sense." Still she rambled on.

"Oh Lord," I prayed. "I need help. Please give me a clue— a path through the confusion." And then the strangest thing happened. Clearly in my mind's eye, I saw a spider's web. It was so real I could have reached out and touched it. Getting anxious, I quietly responded, "Lord, I prayed for help, and you give me this?" Again I waited for divine intervention, only to have the spider's web appear the second time.

"OK, Lord," I said, "Now what?" In my frustration and disappointment for not getting what I perceived was an answer to my prayer, I heard the words, "Go to child."

"What does that mean?" I silently questioned. Then it hit me; children like stories.

I had no idea what to do with this revelation, but when

the woman hesitated, I spoke to her as if she were a child. I leaned forward toward her, and out of my mouth came these words, "Have you ever seen a spider's web?" Startled by the question, she responded hesitantly, "Yes, yes, I've seen a spider's web."

That was her first coherent sentence.

I continued, "Where was the web you saw?"

"It was in our living room. The spiders come when we're using the wood stove. And in the barn—always in the barn."

"Can you describe one to me?" I requested. As she gestured with her hand, descriptive coherent words came from her lips.

I still had no therapeutic plan when I asked, "Have you ever seen a spider in the web?"

"Oh yes, I've seen them lots of times," she replied.

"Well, if you can picture one, I'd like you to color it black," I instructed.

"OK, got it! A black spider in a web." She seemed to be caught up in this story, and I still had no idea where I was headed with the spider's web or what point I would make but decided to trust the words pouring out of my mouth.

"Now, I'd like to give the spider a name. We are going to call it Satan," I said.

"Satan! Why call it Satan? Why are we talking about this spider in a web?" she questioned anxiously.

The answer flowed from my lips with no prior thought. It seemed that God, using my voice, was providing the words.

I was tranquil now and beginning to enjoy this revelation. "Satan is just like a black widow spider who weaves a sticky web in dark hidden places. When an insect touches the spider's web, it is immediately trapped. Once in the web, the insect begins the task of trying to free itself, and just before it breaks out, the spider appears from out of nowhere. It stings its victim with a poisonous venom that creates paralysis, and there the insect's life slowly ebbs away."

"Just like the spider, Satan damages us in our early character forming years. Out of that damage is created a dysfunction in our thinking, feeling, and behaving that will last a lifetime and will effect our most intimate relationships with God, with a marital partner, with children, and with parents."

The woman sat back in her chair and slowly folded her arms. She smiled smugly as though she had just experienced an "ah-ha." "Well then, I know exactly what happened to me," came her answer. She told me about her childhood, which contained every type of abuse: emotional, sexual, and physical. And upon hearing the story, it was a surprise to me that she was functioning on any level at all.

It's the "ah-ha" experience that comes as a result of new knowledge that begins the process of recovery.

"So," she said with new insight, "Given my history, is my current behavior totally off the wall?"

My response served like a glimmer of hope to her. "Given the damages in your childhood, your behavior is quite normal."

"But my behaviors are causing me and my family pain and trouble. What do I do about them? How can I change them?" she pleaded.

My answer seemed to give her hope; "We need to start today to complete the incomplete issues of your past, so you can be freed from your entanglement in Satan's web. You must *uncover* and *face* the past in order to empty yourself of the poisonous emotion that you carry and to fill the empty space with God's complete wisdom and His spirit of love and acceptance."

Your early damage becomes the filter through which you see every experience of life. Your responses to the incidents of the present are driven from the pain of your past. With or without recall of the incident, the resulting damage to your thoughts and feelings drives your behaviors in the present.

Recovery cannot be accomplished overnight or even in a year. It is the work of a lifetime. Actually, the process of sanctification, which is a common Christian concept, is really the process of recovery from the damage Satan did to you early in life, which has created destructive thoughts, feelings, and behaviors in the present.

"Such is the destiny of all who forget God;
so perishes the hope of the godless.
What he trusts in is fragile,
what he relies on is a spider's web.
He leans on his web, but it gives way;
he clings to it, but it does not hold."
Job 8:13-15, NIV

CHAPTER 2

Uncover to Discover

*"Any repressed emotion festers, grows septic,
and contributes to a dis-ease that can only
be healed by allowing the forbidden feeling into
awareness. We can't recover an emotion
whose existence we have denied."*
Sam Klein

Why look at the past to understand the present? It's a legitimate question and one that is asked frequently by those facing the hard work of recovery. Shouldn't we just forget those things that were in the past and keep looking forward toward the future? What has all of that history, especially the things I don't even remember, got to do with today?

An understanding of the physiology of a baby's early brain development will help you to see why your past has such an influence on your present. At five and one-half months gestation, babies in utero begin to absorb mother's emotions into themselves. The emotions that mother experiences, based on the circumstances of her life and the nature of her relationships, are recorded in the mind of the child. If, for example, the mother is unwed and the father has no interest in continuing the relationship with her or refuses to take responsibility and shows no interest in the budding life, the child will interpret the rejection felt by the mother as if it were his or her own rejection. Any emotion the mother feels, whether positive or negative, is passed into the child and recorded as if it had originated with the child. As a result, the child makes its first memories of rejection.

By the seventh month of prenatal development, a baby's unconscious mind has already begun to receive messages from the outside world and become the repository for life's experiences. These messages come primarily through the sense of hearing, and most have an emotional component. Before birth, the child records the sound of mommy's and daddy's voices; even the sounds of sibling's voices or other significant people in relationship with mother are stored in the filing cabinet of the mind.

After birth, there is a significant increase in the number of messages the baby receives, since all five senses are now gathering life-event information. If a baby is touched harshly or experiences physical pain, it's recorded in the child's memory. If a baby sees frightening, angry faces, it's recorded. If a baby tastes or smells unpleasant substances, it's recorded and interpreted as rejection. Every event is recorded as it happens, containing the data from all five senses, plus the emotion the child feels at the time the memory is being made.

The way the human brain works is that when a stimulus comes to us from the outside world, say through our eyes, it is automatically processed, with no commands needed from us. Just as a computer does a global search for everything available related to a certain subject, the mind zips through its recorded memory and rank orders those memories charged with emotion. We will then respond to the initial stimulus in our thinking, feeling, and behaving, based on the memory that is most emotionally charged at that moment.

Emotion is stored in the limbic system, which is in the central part of the brain. A major part of its work is to govern emotional responses to external stimuli. (See chapter 4.)

To understand how the limbic system works, block out external stimuli and then read the word I'm about to give you. Then close your eyes and allow your mind to go wherever it will in response to the word. Give yourself about thirty seconds with your eyes closed before answering the following questions. Are you ready? The word is . . .

Chocolate.

What did you see? Is what you saw connected to a memory of your past? How far back? Most people will go back to a memory from years ago, sometimes childhood. For example, just typing the word *chocolate* sent me (Nancy) back to Christmas at Grandma's. She made heavenly fudge. My mouth waters just at the sight of the word. I can feel the sugary sweet granules and the soft crunch of walnuts. Yummy. She kept the fudge in a pretty old-fashioned tin box, and just when we thought we had eaten the last piece, she would go to a hiding place upstairs under the eaves and bring out one more box. Grandma was a safe, warm, and cuddly place for me, so recall of her brings feelings of love and acceptance and a gentle smile to my face. Even eating a piece of fudge similar to the type she made can create the same feeling of acceptance I felt when she offered me fudge decades ago.

The truth is that whatever memory is charged with the most emotion at the time of stimulation, be it positive or negative, will be the event that will come to the cognizant (thinking) mind.

One day in a seminar we mentioned the stimulus word *strawberry*. A lady responded by immediately breaking into tears. When the lecture was over she said to us privately, "Perhaps you noticed I started to cry when you said the word *strawberry*. I'm seventy-four years old, and when you said the word, I was instantly twelve years old and having one of the worst experiences of my life. I was working for a strawberry farmer, picking berries for the summer. It was nearing the end of the day, and I noticed I was the only one left in the field, so I quickly finished filling my basket and went back to the packing shed to weigh my berries. Suddenly two hands came from behind me and grabbed my breasts. The next thing I knew I was lying on the dirt floor looking up into the face of the farmer and feeling the excruciating pain of sexual violation. I never told the truth of that experience to anyone. Just two years ago my husband passed away. What is overwhelming to me today is that I allowed him to die believing that he was the cause of the sexual difficulties in our marriage. The real truth is that every time I lay beside him and he approached me sexually, I was again a child wincing in pain on the dirt floor. Vivid recall and old fears controlled my sexual response and robbed me of the joy of intimacy."

Our responses, our behaviors, stem primarily from the emotion of old memories and not just the present situation or the emotion of the moment.

Young children respond emotionally to external stimuli, using only the limbic (emotional) system of the brain. They do not have the mechanism to reason from cause to effect, because the filing cabinet of logic, the cerebral cortex, is still developing—and will be until about thirty years of age.

As children approach the age of accountability (approximately twelve years of age), however, there is enough content in the cerebral cortex—in other words, they have created enough memory and have the chemical and physiological mechanism—to begin the process of thinking from cause to effect. In addition, the mechanisms of the brain are more precisely tuned by this age so they are able to link together all pertinent information (logic) before making a choice. The choice now will be based on their emotions *plus* their logic. It is important to note, however, that the decision will be based on *their* logic, not necessarily the logic of parents or other authority figures. Each person's personal experiences impact their logic and thus their choices.

After receiving a stimulus, the brain takes from a split second to a few seconds, functioning at different rates of speed depending on the circumstances of the moment, to sort through the stack of memories containing logical information in order to add it to emotion and thus make a logical, adult decision.

The interesting fact is that adults whose needs were not met or who were damaged in childhood, and whose thinking processes were short-circuited because of the emotional pain, respond automatically on an emotional level using only the limbic system, which controls the response of fight or flight with little or no input of logic. Many do not even know that logic is available for them to use. Unmet needs and damage in the character-forming years create the blind spot.

Many feel the sting of rejection every time circumstances bring up old pain. Perhaps you have found yourself looking for evidence of rejection in your life. The truth is that those who look will find it. Satan has planned it to be so.

If a young child's primary care givers are not meeting the child's needs, the child will react by either withdrawal to thumb sucking, the blankie, or the bottle or outrage by fussing, crying, hollering, or demanding that those needs be filled. An adult child, who because of damage is still responding out of the limbic (emotional) system, will either pout, bury oneself in a computer or TV, anesthetize oneself with alcohol or other drugs to not feel the pain, or will throw temper tantrums, use controlling behaviors, strike out against someone verbally or physically, or turn on the tears. Decisions are made by indecision, circumstances, or by someone else. They end up reacting instead of responding. They shoot from the hip—or the mouth, as the case may be—out of pure impulsive feeling. They live the reactive lifestyle of a child rather than a logically responsive lifestyle of a mature adult.

Perhaps you have found yourself performing or trying to please others in order to gain the acceptance you need because you did not receive it earlier in life. Do you exaggerate your accomplishments so that you can look better in another's eyes? You might be a bragger who needs to be told how good you are. If you have a need to be better than someone else so that you can feel better about yourself, chances are you were rejected in your early years when acceptance is so necessary.

Could it be that adult thinking, which is self-centered, emotionally based, childish in nature, and void of logic and reasoning, is what the Bible refers to as the carnal mind and the enemy of God? Romans 8:6, 7 clearly states, "For to be carnally minded is death, but to be spiritually minded is life and peace. Because the carnal mind is enmity against God; for it is not subject to the law of God, nor indeed can be" (NKJV).

People who are damaged in the first eighteen months of life when trust is supposed to be developed will have difficulty trusting or accepting themselves and others. A deficiency in trust makes it challenging to accept information or knowledge from anyone, and the doubt felt in themselves is translated to a doubting and rejecting of everyone, including God.

How does this information relate to the satanic spider's web? Is this a part of his insidious plan to destroy? Satan can so poison our early lives and pervert our decision-making capability that we continue long after childhood to react with impulsive emotional childish behaviors. In the period from eighteen months to three years of age, a child in a healthy environment will learn autonomy—the ability to make decisions and govern oneself. The damaged child, living in an unhealthy environment, will grow to adulthood wanting its own way, regardless of how illogical it may be. Mature decisions are impossible, as the damaged individual will make decisions based on the emotions of the moment, void of long-range thinking. There are some human beings who are so desperately damaged that they will not receive new information, regardless of the source, will insist that life goes their way, and that their opinions are the only truth. Decisions for new or different truth will not be made by those whose stubborn will has been set by damage. Since this is so, the spiritual experience, based on a knowledge of God and the desire for truth, are stunted. People who refuse to listen are almost always those who have cherished defective hereditary and cultivated tendencies of character and are blind to God's principles and standards.

Let's revisit the original question: *Why look at the past to understand the present?*

We must look at the past, because it is poured in cement, cannot be eliminated, and is the foundation of the life we build. All of the decisions we make are based on the emotions, information, and experiences previously stored in the brain.

As my grandpa (Nancy's) approached his nineties totally blind, needing to be cared for by others, he would sit in his

familiar chair in the bay window of my childhood home, recalling scenes from his boyhood. He would speak of hearing
Billy Sunday preach in Trafalgar Square and would quietly
sing the songs he sang as a boy at those evangelistic meetings. He would recall the days of hard labor in the home of
twelve children and in the mill where he worked as a boy.

As the mind ages, its memories from childhood, especially those that are charged with emotion, are available for
easy recall. Facts and figures cease to have value to the
aged, and relationships with family, childhood chums, and
present family members take first place in importance. Time
is spent reviewing the past, the places seen, the people encountered, and the relationships made. Over and over, the
elderly ask themselves if they have felt accepted and been
an important part of others' lives.

Our childhood memories are the filter through which we
see, hear, smell, taste, touch, and react emotionally throughout our lives. Nearly every painful reaction today is related
to a painful damage or memory from childhood. Experiences,
both positive and negative, carve out the sculpture of the
present and provide the elements for the shape it will take
in the future. Our view of life, determined by our perceptions of the past, influences the decisions we will make in
the present, thus shaping our future.

*It is only by acknowledging the presence and power of
our memories, and then removing the negative emotions attached to painful memories, that we can hope to respond in
an adult manner using the logic of the cerebral cortex. It is
only by facing the past that we can courageously and successfully conquer the present.*

Regardless of how deplorable—how satanic—the memories may be, healing is possible by defusing the emotions of

one's past. Perhaps the most tragic personal history I (Nancy) have ever heard came to light when a friend had her first flashback.

She was a petite little blonde with a bubbly and exciting personality. Her clothing was stylishly chosen and her appearance modern and attractive. Jenny looked the picture of success as she drove around town in her shiny new Chrysler, making friends with influential people.

Jenny was a physician's wife and the mother of two teens. She had a beautifully designed home, and her children were polished and well-behaved. But once in a while, totally out of character for her, she would appear at her husband's office in baggy sweats with unkempt hair and no makeup. From the waiting room, she would call in a childish high-pitched voice, "Honey, Honey" or would come back to the office where I worked and fall apart in a bundle of tears.

Her husband, Burt, was an overworked physician who adored her but did not understand her Jekyll/Hyde personality. Jenny at times seemed very lonely and disconnected from normal relationships. She seemed to be looking for her place, her identity, apart from her husband's world. She took on several jobs, started a business, gave hours of volunteer hospital labor, and had a generous heart of compassion.

Then, just for fun, Jenny and Burt decided to attend a special marriage-seminar weekend. Things were going well at the seminar, and they were enjoying focusing on each other for a change. During one of the presentations, Jenny had a flashback. She had never experienced anything like that before, but in rapid succession one sight after another paraded before her view.

First, there was a little girl about three years of age lying on a marble slab altar, and then she saw twelve men in black hoods and robes standing around her. The little girl was bleeding. Her blood had been drained into a silver challis, which was passed around for each to take a sip. Once the challis had been passed, one after the other took their turn sexually abusing the child.

Jenny was distraught and terribly confused. Where had this scene come from? Why did this come now? Had this been some long-ago horror movie she had seen? Why the fear? The terror? The memory was overwhelming. She bolted from the seminar room to the solitude of their motel room. Burt followed.

Once Jenny's sobbing subsided, she revealed the frightening tale to Burt. For twenty-five years of marriage he had prayed for a key to help them to understand Jenny's behaviors, but surely this far-fetched tale was her imagination run wild.

Suddenly Jenny yanked up the sleeves of her turtleneck; she ran her hand along her exposed arm, stopping at little scars along the way. Bending over, she pulled up her slacks and examined her lower legs. "Haven't we always wondered where these scars on my arms and legs came from? Well, this is the answer, Burt. The little girl is me! These scars are from them draining my blood for the silver challis. And I know who the men were too. I'll name them for you. There was Dr. A and Dr. B. There was Judge C and two lawyers. Their names were D and E. And, Burt, the ringleader of the group was Daddy. I wonder if that's why he's been in a nursing home and totally out of touch since he was fifty-two?"

Burt responded, "Listen, Honey, I've stuck with you through thick and thin, but this is too much. I can't believe this story. How could you make up such a tale?" Very calmly and totally in control, Jenny responded, "For the first time, I have a clue to why my life has been such a roller coaster. I don't like the picture, but the story is true. I'm the little girl, Burt. I'm the little girl!"

When they arrived home, Jenny's sister confirmed the abuse, stating that she had hoped that Jenny had lost the memory of its horror permanently. Jenny set out to prove her story to Burt. She begged him to take her to the town where they had grown up. He agreed but only if a psychologist would go with them. He was afraid Jenny might lose it if she discovered the truth. The three of them drove up and down the street in her old neighborhood. Finally Jenny hollered, "Stop, this is the place!"

They stopped in front of a familiar church, and it was Burt's turn to be shocked. "Not here, Jenny, it can't be here. This is the church I grew up in!"

Totally convinced this was the place, Jenny took a little notebook and a pencil from her purse. "Here, Burt, I'll draw the layout of the church for you."

Carefully she described to the counselor and her husband the details of the building's interior and the circular staircase that led to the room with the marble slab.

They entered the building, and Burt gasped in disbelief. Her description was absolutely accurate. Frightened, they ascended the circular staircase, and Jenny led them to the room where repeatedly in her childhood she had laid on the slab—the victim of satanic ritual abuse.

Burt's tears flowed silently. He was obviously shaken. The evidence was there. He had to believe.

Subsequently Jenny contacted the police and hired a private investigator, who found Jenny's playmate who had lived across the street from her in childhood. This girl confirmed to Jenny that both sets of parents had been involved in a porno ring. They made porno movies using their children and "snuff" movies in which the female is murdered.

Jenny then spoke to her older sister about what she had discovered. Her sister cried, "Oh, God, Jenny, I thought you had forgotten." The truth was that all the girls in Jenny's family had been similarly abused.

So why do we have to look at the past to understand the present? Because out of the past comes historical pieces that complete the puzzle of our lives.

Before Jenny had the revelation about her past, not understanding what was driving her, she had tried to kill herself eight different times. Now, out of Jenny's past came the key to unlock her present behaviors. Had this memory never surfaced and been dealt with, Jenny would certainly have ended her life by her own hand.

Why had this memory surfaced now? She was at the right age and in a safe place.

Programmed into the functions of the brain is an automatic mechanism that is designed to hide painful memories so that they are not accessible for review. This process is called *repression.* It is God's safety mechanism to hide memories from us until we are ready to acknowledge them as ours, receive them, and work through them toward recovery.

Adrenaline in the body is used to help keep the lid on the garbage can in the mind that holds our painful memories. As we come to the age at which the production of adrenaline decreases, there are usually other chemical changes occurring in the body (such as menopausal hormonal changes). If we are parents, often our children are simultaneously in their teenage years, and we are reevaluating our lives. We face the possibilities of career changes and the upcoming empty-nest syndrome, and mothers are often feeling less needed than when the children were little. All these conditions combine to make a set of circumstances that can precipitate emotional turmoil and confusion. Our old and hurtful memories begin to escape from their hiding place. The body is designed to protect itself, so unconsciously we increase the adrenaline level in our bodies by fits of rage, overwork, excessive exercise, hysterical responses, and irrational behaviors. There will come a time, however, when we can no longer contain the memories, and the confusion created makes us think we are going crazy. We find ourselves in crisis.

About this time, we are so vulnerable that we will grasp onto anything we assume will make us feel better, including adulterous affairs, abandonment of the family, or other erratic behaviors. All these things combined create crisis: pandemonium, depression, and self-destructive behaviors. Finally in our desperation, we seek assistance from a friend, counselor, pastor, or anyone who will listen; or feeling hopeless, we consider, or even sometimes attempt, to end it all.

What we need, however, is knowledge. *When we can understand the workings of the mind, the evil intent of Satan, and our own particular damage, we can begin the process of undoing the pain and relieving the pressure.*

As in Jenny's case, God knows how much we can bear and when it is the ideal time to reveal the truth. He will use a safe place where there are supportive individuals to help us through the crisis. For Jenny, the marriage-seminar experience created a loving and supportive atmosphere in which God could return the memory. She was away from home; away from responsibilities, demands, and the incessant ringing of the phone. She and Burt had concentrated time to focus on each other, their lives, and their love. And because Burt had no patients to worry about, he was available to Jenny when she needed him most. Isn't God good?

Jenny was a girl who all of her life had tried to find God. She even considered pastoral ministry. She desperately longed for and pretended to have a relationship with God. But how could she when her own father, who stood in the place of God to her, was the vilest of her abusers.

After the revelation and the beginning of her recovery process, there came an incredible peace upon her that I had never before seen in her. She was relaxed and more consistently adult in her behavior. No longer was she a needy little girl seeking to be filled by everyone around her. She began the process of recovery, which allowed her to grow into the whole and healthy individual God created her to be.

Here is the first step: Before we find pardon and peace, we must have a *knowledge* of ourselves that will result in a repentant attitude. We must recognize our need of Christ's help. We must feel the pain of our wounds before we desire healing.

The reason this is so important is that the damage done to us has stunted and perverted our emotional growth and as Jesus said, "We must be born again." We must die to self, to the sin-filled, carnal nature, and then we must grow up in Him, allowing Him to reparent us and love us into a healthy maturity.

The difference is that this new-birth process begins when we choose it. This time, our birth is not a choice our parents make. It's ours. Unfortunately, it is our desperation, having tried everything we can think of to get ourselves on a positive path, that forces upon us a vulnerable, teachable attitude. We have to come to the point where we realize that what we have been doing doesn't work.

It is in our crisis that we will look to Christ. For many of us, it is not until we hit the bottom of the pit that we look up and like Peter sinking into the sea, we cry, "Lord, save me!" That submissive spirit is the first step toward success. *We must submit to succeed.*

When you recognize your position, incomplete and desperately needy, Jesus offers you all the power of heaven to begin the process of recovery. Why shouldn't He?

- He says, "You are mine" (John 17:6).

- He calls you His son and His daughter (1 John 3:1).

- He says He created you (Ps. 139:13-16).

- He knew you before you were born (Jer. 1:5).

- He died for you (John 3:16).

- He is preparing a home in heaven for you (John 14:1-3).

- You are referred to as Jesus' bride (Rev. 21:9).

- You are loved (Jer. 31:3).

- Nothing can separate you from His love (Rom. 8:35).

- Jesus has redeemed you and forgiven all your sins (Col. 1:14).

- You are a citizen of heaven (Phil. 3:20).

Jesus has everything invested in you. Your value is incomprehensible. He doesn't want to lose you to the spider's web. In fact, He has even given you direct access to His Father through the Holy Spirit (Eph. 2:18) so you have God's power at your fingertips; so much power that if you ask, Jesus can move mountains for you: mountains of guilt, mountains of shame, mountains of disappointment, mountains of rejection, mountains of abusive pain. (See Matt. 17:20.) In addition, Jesus has gone through everything you have gone through. He has been tempted in all the ways you have been, yet He overcame (Heb. 4:15). And through His power, you can too!

Just read Isaiah 53:3 to see what Jesus endured. "He was despised and rejected by men, a man of sorrows, and familiar with suffering. Like one from whom men hide their faces he was despised, and we esteemed him not." Does that sound like something you're going through? Well, He did too.

But there is more. Open your Bible and read for yourself the entire chapter of Isaiah 53, and you will see that Jesus has suffered everything you have suffered—and more! He was rejected by his earthly brothers in His original family, and as a boy, often found it necessary to escape to the more peaceful home of His friend, Lazarus. He carried your sickness, pain, and sorrows; He was punished, stabbed and beaten; He was oppressed and afflicted, and He was finally killed for your sins. Before you were even born, He knew you'd need a Savior and offered Himself as the sacrifice so you could be saved. Your job is simply this: Let Him be your Savior.

The power for Jesus' overcoming came from His Father. The power for your overcoming comes from the same source:

your heavenly Father! By saying Yes to Jesus; all heaven (the Father, the Son, the Holy Spirit, and thousands and ten thousands of angels) becomes your ally against the spider and his web. There is a way to escape. God has not given you "a spirit of fear, but of power and of love and of a sound mind" (2 Tim. 1:7, KJV).

With the power of heaven standing by, you can successfully go through the discovery process, regardless of the initial pain. Wounds don't heal unless they are cleaned out; disinfected. Painful memories are like a boil that must be excised and the infectious pus released in order for healing to commence. You must uncover to recover. You can be born again. The choice is yours.

CHAPTER 3

Garbage In; Garbage Out

"If the brain is a computer,
then it is the only one that runs on glucose,
generates electricity,
and was manufactured by playing in the dirt.
Thank You, Lord."

The brain is an organ in the body just like the heart, liver, or kidneys. As the heart pumps blood bringing vital nutrients to the entire body, the brain regulates the functioning of every organ of the body. It is the master control system; the capital of the body; the seat of all the nervous forces and of mental action; the center of a highly technical mass-communication system. The nerves proceeding from the brain control the body and the vital action of every part of the system.

The mind is the term we use as we talk about part of the functioning of the brain. Its work is to store and process the data that is presented to it. Data comes through information we learn and through everything the eyes see, the ears hear, the nose smells, the skin touches, and the mouth tastes. This information is stored consciously (which is in the thinking, cognizant, awareness, and reasoning portion of our mind) or subconsciously (which is beneath the thinking level of the mind). Simply speaking, the subconscious is a filing cabinet that contains files of information, which at the time of presentation the mind deemed unnecessary at the moment, unimportant or too painful for recall. The limbic system, which is above and surrounding the brain stem, also stores the emotions that we feel in response to everything going on around us. The mind orchestrates incoming stimuli to respond appropriately according to all of the stored data—conscious, subconscious, and emotional.

The subject of whether or not Satan can read minds has been debated for centuries. We are convinced that although he cannot read our minds per se, he knows our heredity and therefore our weaknesses. He knows the early damages that he has inflicted upon us and the resulting emotions. He then listens to our words and watches carefully our responses to various stimuli, and therefore he can calculate in an incredibly accurate way how we are processing our old memories with our current situations, and the result is a fairly reliable "reading" of our minds.

We do know that Satan is the universe's most learned scholar on the human body and brain and its functioning—and his mission is complete control. Since Creation he has been experimenting with the properties of the human mind, trying to link the human mind with his own so he can deceive humans into thinking they are making their own decisions, while in reality they are being led by Satan at his will. He hopes so to confuse the minds of men and women that they are unaware of his control.

Of greatest concern to Satan is seeing to it that the circumstances of our lives are maneuvered in such a way that the mind malfunctions, because he knows Jesus' words are true: "The good man brings good things out of the good stored up in his heart [mind], and the evil man brings evil things out of the evil stored up in his heart [mind]. For out of the overflow of his heart [mind] his mouth speaks" (Luke 6:45, NIV; parentheses supplied). In other words, our responses are based on whatever emotionally laden data is stored in our minds.

Our only recourse against Satan's deceptions is to become students of the mind. We must study the influence of the mind upon the body and of the body upon the mind and the laws by which they are governed. And in so doing we can begin to understand ourselves and do the work of recovery that will result in pardon and peace. Christ can only save us if we realize we are sinners. He came "to heal the brokenhearted, to preach deliverance to the captives, and recovering of sight to the blind, to set at liberty them that are bruised" (Luke 4:18, KJV). But "they that are whole need not a physician" (Luke 5:31). Here's the answer: We must know our real condition, or we won't feel our need of Christ's help. We must feel the pain of our wounds, or we won't desire Christ's healing.

Since the mind is so important to our day-to-day functioning and to our spiritual present and future, it is important that we examine its function—at least in a simplistic way.

Not every scientist agrees about the number of memory cells the mind contains, but estimates run between one and three trillion (1,000,000,000,000-3,000,000,000,000). Each has the capacity to store the entire set of the *Encyclopedia Britannica.* The mind is taking in messages from the outside environment through all of the senses at the rate of about one hundred thousand per second. These messages are selectively kept and filed or deleted by the mind. Much of the information taken in through the senses is not retained because the mind has its own ability to delete data it deems as unimportant. The mind is like a powerful computer, storing and filing data during all of our waking moments and at times during sleep.

Why do you suppose that God would create a mind with such infinite capacity? Even if we would live 150 years, we would use up very few of our memory cells. This question is often asked as we teach a seminar, and it is interesting to hear the responses of participants. Almost always someone will call out "because God created us to live eternally." Obviously we will continue to learn throughout eternity—and God won't have to perform brain surgery to make that happen.

Picture a stack of CDs (compact discs) set one on top of the other, all in their plastic jackets and labeled with title, content, and performer. This is a simplistic and imaginary view of the memories in the mind. Stimuli come to us from the outside world and sometimes even from our own minds. Outside stimuli come to us through the senses, with sight and sound being the most powerful stimuli. At the speed of light, our mind processes through the entire stack of memories. It pulls from the stack those memories that relate to the stimulus, rank ordering them according to their emotional charge at that moment. The memory with the most emotion, either positive or negative, will orchestrate the whole person to respond to that memory in preference to the reality of the moment. We know that old memories are stored in detail and can be relived, because scientists have used a tiny probe to touch specific areas of the brain and immediately the patient relives the memory with all details and senses included as if it were happening at that moment.

Those memories charged with pain from the past will override all other memories including the present stimulus. It would seem, then, that we tend to live in the past more than the present, wouldn't it? Our behaviors are more reactions than they are actions based on present reality. Even a current emotion can activate an old subconscious memory that may have laid dormant for years, setting in motion a chain of memories that will assist us to find missing pieces to the puzzle of our lives.

While at a religious convention, someone asked us for a written description of one of the seminars we teach. Later in our motel room, I (Nancy) started up the computer and called up the appropriate file for filling the request. I decided to revise the description we had previously written. I worked at the computer for about a half hour, and Ron read quietly, reclining on the bed. All of a sudden, what looked to be Egyptian hieroglyphics appeared on the screen. "Oh no," I sighed, "I've done it again!" In desperation I asked Ron, "What have I done this time? Please help me!"

Ron came and stood behind me looking over my shoulder at the computer screen and then said to me, "I don't know how you do it, Girl. I surely have no idea how you came up with this. Get up and I'll see what I can do."

Whether it was there or not, I heard the disgust in his voice. Begrudgingly I got up from my desk chair, flopped myself on the end of the bed, heaving a sigh of disgust at my own stupidity, and I felt my jaws tighten and my teeth press together. I was angry, and I knew it. But why? Was I really that angry at myself? Or was it at Ron—when he was only trying to rescue me? I didn't like the feeling. It frightened me. Quietly I prayed, "Lord, when have I felt like this before? Please show me where the rage comes from."

In just moments a very old scene passed before me. I was thirteen and a freshman in high school. We had been given our first essay assignment in science class. I was sitting at the kitchen table with my new portable typewriter in front of me. I had filled about two-thirds of the page when my father came up from the basement workshop. He approached me, asking, "What are you doing, Poode?" (Poode was his pet name for me.)

"Just typing this term paper for science class," I replied.

Daddy stood behind me, reading over my shoulder what I had typed. A moment or two went by before he reached for the paper in the typewriter and ripped it out. He said, "They'll never accept that garbage. Just get up; I'll do it." Resentfully I watched as my father typed my entire paper, knowing that I would have to turn in his work instead of mine. Now that I look back on this incident, I realize that Dad was just trying to help me. It was probably his way of saying, "I'll help you because I love you." But the message I got was of *rejection*. His actions said, "You're stupid and can't do anything right. Why do I always have to fix things you mess up?"

This old memory was my answer to the rage of the moment! I knew that the way I felt with Ron sitting at the computer was exactly what I had felt when Dad took my place at the typewriter. The anger then became the rage now. I just knew that I couldn't do it right, and I was never good enough, nor would I ever be. I was a disappointment to my father and I knew it, and now I was a disappointment to Ron. Approval from the man in the present was as important as approval from the man in the past. The fact that Ron loved me and was only trying to help me after I asked him to had not been taken into account. The stimulus was the words *Get up, and I'll see what I can do*. Those words took me back almost forty years, and I responded from the internal anger that had been smoldering there without my realizing it.

As soon as the memory returned and I had recognized its origin, I assumed that Ron probably detected my anger. So I chose to share the truth with him. "You know, Honey, a few minutes ago when you told me to get up from the chair so you could fix the mess I had made, I was instantly angry."

Ron replied, "I know you were."

"Well," I continued, "I didn't like the feeling, so I asked the Lord to show me when I had felt this way before. What flashed before me was a scene when I was thirteen years of age . . ." and I told him the story, assuring him that the anger was not directed at him but at my father and myself. It was an old memory, a CD from the past, being replayed and re-interpreted as the present.

By sharing the truth with Ron I was able to acknowl-edge that I was really responsible for the anger, not Ron. He would no longer need to question whether or not he had done something to upset me. I also gave a strong message to my own mind; a message of completion and of confession. Completion that the appropriate memory returned and that I, because I was able to recognize its impact on my life, could remove the powerful negative emotional charge from the old memory, thus neutralizing its affect on the present. "Then you will know the truth, and the truth will set you free" (John 8:32, NIV). In addition, I had taken a giant step toward self-understanding by the confession of this memory to Ron, which then assisted Ron in understanding me more fully.

Human beings are a composite of all past memories. Com-bined, these memories create our thoughts and our feelings out of which come our behaviors.

(Ron) In the seminar setting I often illustrate the power of past memory by asking someone in the audience to come forward and sit in a folding chair where everyone can see. Usually the person willingly sits in the chair, even though they have no idea why I am asking them to do this. After sitting there for a few seconds, I begin to question them, "Suppose you had come to sit in this chair and it collapsed beneath you and you ended up on the floor, with the audience laughing at you. We help you up off the floor, and it's break time. We return from break. Once more I invite you to come and have a seat, assuring you the chair has now been fixed. Would you come?"

My participant usually answers, "Well, maybe if I tested the chair to make sure it wouldn't collapse again."

Then I say, "Suppose it collapses once more? This time you are not just embarrassed but enraged that I would set you up for another fall. If the next day I would ask you to come and sit once again in the chair, assuring you I had taken it to a repair shop and now it was guaranteed to support you, would you sit in it?"

Almost all participants respond, "No way! The first time I could excuse it, but the second really made me look like a fool, and I could no longer trust you."

Then I make the point that we are a composite of all our past memory. To a person sitting in the audience the second day, who had not seen what happened before, the refusal of someone to sit in the chair would appear irrational. They would ask, "What would be the big objection to sitting in the chair?"

Our chair-sitting participant would reply, "Well, you don't know what happened yesterday!" Because we do not know or understand the yesterdays in the lives of others, we can't judge the behavior of others. *Past history dramatically affects present behavior.*

(Nancy) Once in a high school seminar, I asked the students to identify where their minds took them when I said the word *chocolate*.

One student responded, "I saw a giant Hershey bar!"

"Is that your favorite chocolate?" I asked.

"Oh yes!" came the response. "I always buy Hershey's when I have a hankering for something sweet."

"What memory of yours is connected to a Hershey bar?" I asked. "Was there something special about it? Can you recall your first Hershey bar?"

"When I was little we had a candy store near our house. Once a week I could go there with my dad, and he would buy a Hershey bar for me and one for himself." I noticed redness around his eyes and a softness came to his voice that wasn't there before, so I pursued the issue further. "Do you still go with your dad once a week for a Hershey bar?"

Quietly he answered, "Nope. My parents divorced when I was seven, and I see my dad maybe once a year, if I'm lucky. Never thought about it before, but maybe I like Hershey bars, 'cause it reminds me of better times when Dad was part of my life."

No doubt, there were those in the room who had also noticed this young man's tears and thought them quite inappropriate, until they knew the complete truth of their classmate's loss. Often, we take attention away from our personal issues by focusing our attentions on others, making value judgments and character-demeaning remarks. The Bible terms this behavior "evil surmising." How thoughtless it is to do this when we don't know or understand the history behind the behavior. It's so easy to spotlight someone else's faults and ignore our own. The Bible speaks of it as seeing the sliver in another's eye and missing the log in our own. (See Matt. 7:5.) Usually we do this because we do not know how to fix our pain. The result is that we continue to be controlled by our pain, rather than experiencing the freedom of self-understanding. We must and we can recognize the pain we carry and the resulting unhealthy things we do. This is a vital ingredient in the process of spiritual and emotional growth.

Memories are not actually stacked one upon the other but are fragmented with each sense going to its own area of the brain to be stored. Each memory contains all the senses. But when memories are returned, they may be incomplete. For example, one adult woman who had been a victim of severe childhood abuse awakened in the middle of the night with a sense of panic. She felt all the emotion of impending doom, but the only accompanying sense was that of smell. She smelled beer. She quickly got out of bed, washed her face in cold water, blew her nose, and did everything she could to get rid of the smell. She asked herself, "How is it possible to smell beer when there is no alcoholic beverage in this home and never has been? Where is it coming from?" Throughout the next few months she awakened in the middle of the night with the same sense of panic but accompanied with another sensory perception, such as pins and needles around her mouth. It took four months for the final picture to be revealed: the face of her drunken father, who had incested her from very early childhood to her teen years.

Memories can return by the stimulus of a smell, a taste, a sound, a sight, or a touch. The sense of sight is the most powerful as it relates to stimulating memory, even though it takes milliseconds longer for the response. When sight is stimulated, the retina picks up the image and has to send it through various connections before it reaches the visual cortex, where sight is stored. The senses of smell and taste are directly connected to the limbic system, where emotion is housed. Smell is a particularly powerful and rapid stimulant for recall. Frequently stimulation of taste or smell is the sense that activates a sleeping or repressed memory. For years, I (Nancy) enjoyed the fragrance of lavender. I then learned that lavender is a tranquilizing fragrance, and I assumed that was the reason for the positive, comforting emotion I experienced when smelling it. One day in an out-of-town herbal market, I saw a display of natural fragrances, and there were several items labeled English Lavender. I twisted open the talcum powder top, and as I sniffed, the clear picture of my grandma stood before me. Immediately my eyes became tear-filled as I recalled her fragrance and her tender words of affection to me.

When a memory returns, it can do so in its entirety with all the senses and emotions intact, or it may be just a fragment of the memory that surfaces, stimulated by one of the senses.

(Ron) I had an experience where a recalled memory helped me understand why for a dozen years I had acted so bizarre every time Nancy poured hot water into a teacup.

It all started on the Sunday evening after we moved into our first apartment. I was a college student, and Nancy was helping me with Freshman Composition, which to me was worse than Greek. To ease the tension of Nancy's struggle to get me to understand that a verb is an action word, she suggested that we have a hot drink.

I agreed that a cup of tea would be delightful, so she got up from the floor where we'd been studying and went to the kitchen just a few feet away. After the kettle began to whistle, she removed it from the stove and began to pour the water into the cup. She was bringing me a "gift" of love. I knew that, but my response was bazaar. I growled a disgusted "Thanks."

"What's wrong, Honey?" she questioned.

"Nothing!" I snapped in response.

She pursued with "Well, just a few minutes ago before I went into the kitchen, you were fine. Now that I've returned with the tea, you seem angry."

"I'm NOT angry," I shouted.

She left it there, afraid to aggravate further anger.

Repeatedly during the next twelve years, I responded to her in anger when she brought me a hot beverage, even though I would ask for the drink. It was a puzzle to both of us!

On one such occasion, I shouted to Nancy as she poured, "I don't like that noise!" This time there was at least a connection. The anger must be coming from the noise, but what noise? Nancy decided to pursue the subject.

"Just what noise don't you like?" she asked as she approached the living room, cup in hand.

"The noise of the liquid being poured into a cup," I responded, with less anger than before. "It gives me the 'willies.' It's a very uncomfortable, creepy feeling, and I have no idea what it's connected to," I said.

"I suppose that in time it'll come to you," she responded and let the subject drop. She knew that backing me into a corner was only asking for more rage. I would come out of that emotional corner smashing anything in my path and hurling verbal insults. Blame for the incident, and any other uncomfortable things in my life, would be dumped on Nancy.

For twelve years, my wife danced around my reaction, until the answer was revealed to me. It came at an occasion when I heard the sound of boiling beverage being poured into a cup and smelled the freshly brewed coffee. When the sense of smell, which is directly connected to the seat of emotions, was stimulated along with the sound, a visual picture flashed up in my memory. Tears welled in my eyes. Immediately my anger switched to the childish pain of rejection.

I told Nancy, "I see myself pressed against the inside of my bedroom door. It's a Saturday night, and I have been locked in my bedroom so that my parents could entertain their friends around the dining room table just outside my door. The routine was that when the doorbell rang, which was almost every Saturday night, my father would grab me by the ear and drag me to my bedroom. 'You stay in here, Butch,' he would say as he locked the door with an old skeleton key. I then spent the next three or four hours trying to peek out the keyhole to see what the adults were laughing at, certain that it was me. I could smell the pastries my mother had spent the day baking, without giving me a bite, and the strong coffee that Europeans drink." Suddenly I knew why I was angry. The smell of the coffee and the sound of pouring liquid had brought it all back.

I sobbed out the story and expressed the pain I felt as a child, and continued to feel as an adult. Finally I was in touch with the emotion and the damage that had caused this bizarre behavior.

Did that mean I would never again respond with anger at the stimulus of hearing water poured? No indeed! The anger came up for the next few years, but each time when hearing the sound, I would say, "I don't like that noise, but that was then and this is now. I am an adult. I no longer have to be a little boy locked in a room. I am loved and accepted in my home."

The more times I repeated the truth, the easier it was for me to believe it! Occasionally the old anger surfaced, but I had created so many positive records to replace the negative that I was no longer plagued with the memory. My mind created a new pathway; a new set of positive CD's. So now when the stimulus comes, I can choose to respond positively, in a healthy adult way. My tendency now is to affirm my wife rather than blaming her for everything.

Actually, the power to choose a positive response comes from the Holy Spirit, whose work it is to transfer heavenly power to us, especially in times of great need. Here is where we are different from Pavlov's German shepherds, who merely reacted by salivating to the sound of a bell that had become associated with a piece of meat. Even though the meat was not there in the later experimenting, the dogs still responded from the *previous* memories. It was a stimulus which, without thinking, brought forth a conditioned response. We do not have to be stuck in that cycle of repetitious self-defeating behaviors!

As humans, we are given the gift of choice. As Christians, we are given heavenly Power to make the *right* choice. Our work is to understand the driving force of our own past memories, process through them, removing the painful emotions, and then fill our minds with positive and uplifting messages.

In this context, it is easy to understand why the apostle Paul said, "Rejoice in the Lord always. I will say it again: Rejoice! Let your gentleness be evident to all. The Lord is near. Do not be anxious about anything, but in everything,

5—BELONGING

by prayer and petition, with thanksgiving, present your requests to God. And the peace of God, which transcends all understanding, will guard your hearts and your minds in Christ Jesus. Finally, brothers, whatever is true, whatever is noble, whatever is right, whatever is pure, whatever is lovely, whatever is admirable—if anything is excellent or praiseworthy—think about such things" (Phil. 4: 4-8, NIV). Dwelling on these positive scripts can renew our minds.

When our minds are clogged with painful feelings from past injustices done to us, we are not free to receive spiritual truth or accept the recovery God offers, enabling us to bring a halt to our driven behaviors. Once we unclog our minds of the emotional "goo," we are open to receive the healing Christ offers and to make adult decisions based on logic and reason, as well as healthy emotional input.

All the power of the universe is available to us between the stimulus and our response to it. Jesus knows that Satan is trying to get control of the minds of men and women, and He's ready to help all who call upon Him for help. He is not willing that any should perish. (See Matt. 18:14.) So He has placed the power of heaven within the reach of His children. While Satan is busy endeavoring to control the mind, there is a place of safety from his darts. It's in the presence of Jesus.

At the point of our weakness or temptation, we have the power to make a choice, providing we have the right information. We can choose to respond in an adult and Christlike manner rather than being controlled and in submission to Satan's game. He attempts to force us into automatic responses to the stimuli that "pulls up" our early damage and pain. If we do not understand the origin of our feelings and thoughts, we are inclined to respond automatically, just like Pavlov's German shepherds.

By doing so, he has caused us to sin, thus damaging ourselves and others again. *Garbage in; garbage out!* He blinds us to the truth of his cunning ways, and we conclude that we are hopelessly incorrigible, filled with sin and lost eternally. When he can push us to this conclusion, we will cease our striving for God and settle for being "lost."

Grace is the answer. Webster defines grace as "the unmerited, divine assistance of God for the sanctification and regeneration of mankind." It is the assistance of the power of God, meted out through the Holy Spirit, and poured into those who are teachable and anxious to receive it. Grace is what happens between the stimulus and our response, so our painful memories don't control our actions. Grace turns childish emotional responses into mature Christlike responses. We have the help of all heaven, so that we can grow up to maturity and be made new, so that we can become participants with Christ, responding in concern for others rather than in protection of self.

God desires that we be abundantly happy and live in peace, and that peace is promised to us as a gift from God that comes to us through the indwelling of His Holy Spirit. In a promise made to His disciples prior to His crucifixion, Jesus differentiated between the peace the world gives and that which He promises.

"Peace I leave with you; my peace I give you. I do not give to you as the world gives. Do not let your hearts be troubled and do not be afraid" (John 14:27, NIV).

How can you be a recipient of this peace? God has provided the way for the alleviation of the pain. It is through the following triple A plan:

- Acquisition of knowledge
- Application of this knowledge to ourselves
- Actively following God's plan of recovery

If we do not choose to follow the plan, the garbage Satan has put into our early lives will result in garbage seeping out of our present lives, thus poisoning relationships and causing further pain and rejection.

CHAPTER 4

Virus in the Software

"Experience, particularly in childhood sculpts the brain."
Daniel Goleman

You may ask yourself, "What problems do I have? Sure there are obstacles in my life, but I can bulldoze my way through. I can just get on my knees and pray about it, or I'll just forget about it and pretend there is no pain! If I don't think about it, then maybe it will go away." But that's wishful thinking!

If the solution is as simple as just steeling yourself against past injustices or praying about them and having the memories magically disappear, then why are there so many discouraged, angry, frustrated, depressed, and lonely people in this world? Why does rage finally erupt like an unsuspecting volcano, hurting innocent people in its path? The reason is, it's not so simple!

Too many people join churches hoping for a miracle and then end up blaming God when church membership doesn't make their problems go away. Many are spending fortunes on doctor visits, medications and psychotherapy, and years later they are not appreciably better.

There are no quick fixes. We are a fast-food/TV generation that has become accustomed to seeing major problems solved in sixty minutes or less, complete with commercials. And we expect the same in our own lives. The fact is that God requires that we confess our sins and humble our hearts before Him, and at the same time we should have confidence in Him as a tender Father who will not forsake those who put their trust in Him. We do not realize how many of us walk by sight and not by faith. We believe what we see but do not appreciate or appropriate the precious promises given to us in His Word. And as a result, we dishonor God most when we distrust what He says and question His truthfulness.

Our inability to have the confidence, trust, and reliance upon God and His promises is directly related to the satanic damage done to us in childhood either deliberately or by our needs being unmet. When our emotional development is arrested, we become trapped in childhood thinking, feeling, and behaving, so we believe only what we see, and then only if it suits our purposes.

In order to be truly healed, we must comprehend the full scope of our wounds and be willing to uncover the experiences of our lives where the pain was inflicted.

To discover the path toward freedom, we must revisit the memory. Prayer is important, but it is not the only component to healing. We ourselves have a work to do.

For some this is frightening because they fear discovering unknown facts and potential agony that may be hidden in the dark recesses of the mind. There is a psychological law that must be understood here: *Fear paralyzes.* It is our fear of the unknown that prevents us from moving forward toward maturity. Also for some, our behaviors resulting from the pain have become our identity. We are known as angry, sarcastic, timid, or withdrawn people. If we were to undo past pain, then who would we be? Change is frightening. Fear restricts and imprisons us. It binds us to the object or persons we fear, preventing growth and change. We stay trapped in imaginary sights and sounds and expectations of doom.

Fear prevents us from doing the work of facing the truth and cleaning up our past. Some have gone to the extent of pulling Bible passages out of context and misquoting inspirational writings, to prove to themselves and others, that the work of recovering from Satan's damages is not necessary. For example, the New Testament injunction "forgetting those things that are behind, and reaching forth unto those things which are before, I press toward the mark for the prize" (Phil. 3:13,14) has been used as justification for avoiding the work of cleaning up personal garbage cans of hurtful memories. In that text Paul speaks of forgetting the *sins* of our past and confidently pressing toward promised salvation. He is not speaking of forgetting the open wounds of our past that need to be disinfected so healing can proceed from the inside out. He is referring to not dwelling on guilt and admonishing us to look toward a positive future. The quick fix of a simple Band-Aid, like manly muscle, sheer grit, or even repetitious prayer, just won't get the results needed because none of these methods meet the criteria for recovery that God's Word teaches.

Character improvement, which is the sum total of our thoughts and feelings, takes daily determination and effort. When we try to separate ourselves from our sinful habits, such as fault-finding, judging, criticism, greed, and envy, it may at times seem that we are tearing ourselves all to pieces. But if we want to have mature Christlike characters, this is the very *work* that we must do in order to become fit temples for the indwelling of the Holy Spirit. God doesn't want us to have weak, feeble characters. He doesn't want us to remain helpless and ignorant. Instead, God wants us to put on the whole armor of faith and *fight valiantly the battle* against sin and self. (See Ephesians 6:11.) And after we have truly repented of our sins and done all that we can to overcome them, which includes dealing with the painful memories of sin inflicted upon us, the result is, hopefully, a calm un-yielding trust in Jesus, our Savior.

Here enters a concept we first introduced in chapter 2 and will expand upon later in chapter 9. It's a significant piece of information that explains why Satan would damage very young children. *Trust is developed in the first eighteen months of life.* Trust comes to us as infants as we lay in the arms of a nurturing and affectionate mother and recognize that this is a very safe place. It comes through repetition of that same experience over and over until the picture of mother is synonymous with safety and comfort. Trust comes when we realize that daddy's arms are strong enough to hold us and to not fail us in times of need. We feel trust when the gnawing pain of hunger is filled at mother's breast or when the discomfort of soiled diapers is relieved by the tender cleansing that parents provide. Trust is embedded in us as we feel the assurance of our own cozy crib and soft blankie and the pleasant smell of mother. As we learn that our mother's velvet hands and our father's powerful ones provide soothing and protective touch, we come to trust them implicitly.

The child who does not have these vital relational elements will grow to be untrusting, totally self-reliant, distant individuals who seek to control the world and relationships, which are believed to be untrustworthy, just like their primary care givers.

The other emotional tasks to be accomplished as the child grows, such as autonomy, initiative, industry, and identity (based on Eric Erickson's life span developmental tasks), will be severely impacted because the foundational task of trust was never developed.

You may not be cognizant of a painful childhood memory. You may say to yourself, "I had a wonderful childhood. I had perfect parents who adored me and spent meaningful time playing and caring for me." You may not recall any physical, emotional, or sexual damages; however, you may notice that you have difficulty committing 100 percent in a marriage or sharing your thoughts and feelings with others for fear they will reject you. You may be prone to over-commitment; a workaholic driven to get things done. You may have a perfectionistic bent that leads you to sacrifice your health or relationships for the accomplishment of projects. You may be laden with guilt because of a sexual drivenness you can't explain that controls the major portion of your thinking time. You may be a sad or critical individual who spends hours judging yourself and others. These are all consequences of Satan's unhealthy scripts that he has imposed upon you some time early in life. It may be so subtle that there is no one memory or traumatic incident on which you can blame your thoughts or behaviors, but they affect your life just the same. (See chapter 8.)

It is important to understand that behaviors do not develop out of a vacuum. There is always a causative element, such as a physical ailment or an emotional wound that causes dysfunctional behaviors.

Take, for example, the parents who made a counseling appointment with us because they had great concerns about the recent behavior of their nine-year-old son, Bradley. For their first visit we asked the parents to come to our counseling office without their son.

The mother reported, "Our nine year old has always been a model child, but lately he has been doing something that makes no sense at all. He has begun urinating in the corners of rooms in our house. It's disgusting. And how am I ever going to get rid of the smell? He has been potty trained for years, and there's no reason for this behavior!" It was obvious that she was both upset and annoyed by having to continually clean the corners of their wall-to-wall carpeting.

The father added some pertinent information, "We have taken Bradley to his pediatrician, and he can't find anything wrong with him physically. He suggested that we seek help from a counselor."

"We admire your concern and are always pleased when a parent leaves no stone unturned to discover the cause of a child's sudden, unusual behavior," we encouraged. "We will do our best to help."

They pressed for answers. "Well, what shall we do for him? What would prompt a child to do such a thing?"

"Tell us more about what's happening in your home. For example, how large your family is and how many people live in your home? What are the ages of his siblings? How long have the two of you been married?" We pressed for more information in an attempt to determine if there were circumstances present that might precipitate such behavior. We questioned about the atmosphere in their home, the quality of their marriage, and any recent conflicts that could have created stressors in their son.

Within a very short time, as their comfort level increased with us, it became quite evident that the major contributing factor to Bradley's behavior was the state of his parents' marriage. It seems that there had always been some level of conflict in the home, but for the previous six weeks or so discussions of separation or divorce had surfaced within the son's hearing.

Several weeks of counseling passed with only the parents coming to sessions. The concentration of our work with them was focused on resolving the two major conflicts that the parents were having with each other. At the beginning of one session, the mother exploded in anger. She was incensed because they had never been instructed to bring the boy to counseling. "We didn't come here for marriage counseling," she growled. "We came because of a problem with our son! When are you ever going to see him?"

"Well, to answer that question, I must ask you another question," we replied. "Is your son still urinating in corners instead of in the toilet?"

"Well . . . , no he's not," she snapped.

"That is surely great news!" we exclaimed, and then added, "Sometimes children will be in so much pain and stress because of home conflict that they will unconsciously develop a behavior so weird that the attention will be taken from the conflicts and placed on them. In that way they hope to get the parents to agree about what to do with them and hopefully forget their fight. "Tell us," we added, "when was the last time Bradley urinated in a corner of the house?"

"Oh, I can't remember for sure, but I think it was sometime about two and a half weeks ago," the father replied.

"We hope you understand that having eliminated the possibilities of a medical problem, it was logical for us to investigate the emotional stress in the child's life," we explained.

Conflict between parents is displayed in the dysfunctional behaviors on the part of the children. Often children are so distressed with the relational conflict in the home that they will attempt to "fix" it by becoming the focus of the conflict, thus creating parental agreement in order to "fix" the child. The internal drive toward wholeness and harmony is so strong that many will do whatever they deem necessary to create that place of comfort and safety. In this case, the child's diversionary tactics, combined with the counseling his parents received, provided the beneficial answer that everyone involved needed.

What begins in our character-forming years determines the direction of our lives. When our thoughts and feelings are damaged in our primary character-forming years, which are from the beginning of the third trimester of pregnancy until the end of the seventh year of life, something quite dramatic happens to our emotional development. This has been identified with several different labels, such as arrested development, emotional immaturity, the adult child, or the inner child, yet each title refers to the result of Satan's damage upon a life. Satan has indeed set loose a virus in the software, which dwarfs and perverts the better nature of individuals and creates hardhearted and selfish characters.

When children are neglected or their needs go unmet, or when they are damaged early in life, often they cease to develop emotionally at the same pace as they do physically. While the body and its functions matures, the emotions cease their progress. A physical adult can easily be an emotional child. In such cases, the world revolves around the individual, and all those in relationship with him/her are expected to meet all the needs of the individual at all times. Emotional dwarfs expect that all of life should go the way they choose— no one else matters. Meals are served at the moment they want them, the entire household schedules itself around them, and they always get their own way—or else. The "or else" can involve childish temper tantrums displayed any place and any time. Everyone is required to be responsible to them, but they take no responsibility for themselves or others.

In the introduction of Daniel Goleman's best-selling book entitled *Emotional Intelligence,* he states, "Our genetic heritage endows each of us with a series of emotional set-points which determines our temperament. But the brain circuitry involved is extraordinarily malleable; temperament is not destiny . . . The emotional lessons we learn as children at home and at school shape the emotional circuits, making us more adept—or inept—at the basics of emotional intelligence. This means that childhood and adolescence are critical windows of opportunity for setting down the essential emotional habits that will govern our lives" (xiii).

Psychological experts agree that children damaged before the beginning of their eighth year will *cease their emotional maturing* near the age at which the damage takes place. These children may grow up to be physical adults, but in the area of emotions and adult responses they remain as little children. Their growth potential is directly related to their teachability and their willingness to do the personal work required for healing.

If you are one of these "children," it is important that you allow yourself to be vulnerable to God's leading. In compassion He will bring to your mind what you need from your past to understand why you act the way you do. If God feels it is necessary for you to have a memory in order to make progress in your recovery, He will return to you what you need in order to complete the recovery process. He may do it in stages, slowly as your mind can tolerate the information, or He may do it in one quick revelation. Your willingness to be open and teachable is God's permission to begin a maturing and sanctifying process within you.

The first step is the acquisition of knowledge. Let's return to take another look at the brain and the way emotions are processed.

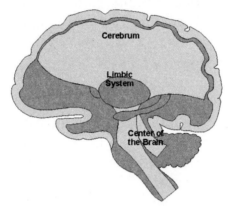

There are three primary areas of the brain that we need to be concerned with as we discuss the healing of painful memories. A cross section of the brain reveals that these appear to be intimately layered one over the other. The center of the brain includes the spinal cord, the brain stem, and the midbrain. It houses unlearned, pre-programmed sets of behaviors or bodily functions, such as breathing, heartbeat, sleeping, waking, and consciousness. It is the first area of the brain to develop and is fully functional at birth, or life would not be possible.

The second most common part of the brain is the cerebrum, which is divided anatomically into two halves known as the left and right hemispheres. It is composed of very elaborate tissue containing millions of neurons per square inch and is about one-eighth of an inch thick. This part of the brain is capable of solving very detailed and complicated problems. The functions contained in these two hemispheres are all the visual processes, hearing, body sensations, intentional motor control, reasoning, cerebral thinking, decision making, purposeful behavior, language, and nonverbal ideas.

Nestled between these two well-known areas of the brain, and intricately connected, is the limbic system. Although it has not gotten much press, it is by far the most important as it relates to the understanding of memory and the recovery process. It is the center of our emotions and our emotionally related behaviors. Here's how Ned Herrmann, president of the American Creativity Organization, describes the limbic system in his book *The Creative Brain:* "Although considerably smaller than the cerebral hemispheres in terms of cortex, the limbic system plays an enormous role in our functioning. If blood supply is a significant indication of importance, then it is worth noting that the limbic system has one of the richest blood supplies in the entire body. And no wonder! The limbic system regulates eating, drinking, sleeping, waking, body temperature, chemical balances, such as blood sugar, heart rate, blood pressure, hormones, sex, and emotions. It's also the focus of pleasure, punishment, hunger, thirst, aggression and rage . . . It is physiologically positioned to mediate brain activity that occurs both below and above it. And it does! It can, for example, overwhelm rational thought with emotional energy and thus completely neutralize logical modes of processing.

"In addition to controlling our emotions, the limbic system also contributes to our cognitive processing. It is now known to be essential to the learning process because it plays a vital role in transferring incoming information into memory" (33).

While the limbic system is the center for emotions and emotional responses, it is also capable of storing emotionally charged memory and perceiving incoming stimuli on its own, apart from the logic or reasoning of the cerebrum. In other words, this emotional switchboard, located deep in the brain, is the power behind our reception of emotional messages, our interpretation of them, and the responses we generate and deliver as a result. It does not, however, have the ability to put the feelings or emotions into words.

The different parts of the brain, even though they have their own purpose, work in cooperation with each other. The circuitry is often so closely linked that one would think they were part of the same system. For example, the hypothalamus, located beneath the thalamus and deep in the brain, works in concert with the limbic system. Richard M. Restak, M.D., the author of *New York Times'* best-selling book, *The Brain*, says, "The hypothalamus is also the command center for a host of complex motivational states: fatigue, hunger, anger, placidity." In addition, the hypothalamus takes control of food intake, endocrine levels, water balance, sexual rhythms, and the autonomic nervous system. "In all, the hypothalamus is an orchestrator for the behaviors that accompany emotional states."

When we are exposed to a stimulus, the brain automatically accesses its memory files and activates the command for a global search, looking for all past memories related to the present stimulus. These memories are listed on the computer screen of the mind in a split second, and just that quickly, we respond based on the memory that is most charged with emotion at that moment. Why would this be? Why would the past dictate the present?

Individuals who have experienced rejection in childhood, whose memories of being ignored, untouched, or chosen last are so plentiful and hurtful, have instant access to that pain. The memory is supercharged with the emotion felt at the time the memory was made, and contains very little logic because of the underdeveloped state of the cerebral cortex (which houses logic) in early childhood.

(Ron) When I was a Cub Scout going on a weekend camping trip, I asked my mother to care for a little rabbit I had won at the theater. When I returned home the bunny was dead, and for a lifetime I blamed my mother for that loss. I thought that she had neglected it, just as I had been neglected as a baby. In my early forties, on a fact-finding mission about my childhood that I processed with my mother, she reminded me of the fact that she had shown me the two red dots on the rabbit's neck when I came home and found it dead. "Do you remember that I turned the rabbit over with a stick, pointed to those dots and explained to you that a weasel had gotten into the hutch and killed your bunny?" she asked.

I had totally forgotten that fact, but the picture of it returned the instant she mentioned it. I had based my blame of mother on the emotion I felt as a child. That emotion was based on the rejection I felt from her from before my birth. (See chapter 6.)

We are a composite of all previous experiences in our lives. Even repressed memories housed in the subconscious mind play a dramatic part in the decisions we make today. It is the content of the subconscious mind that often drives our current behaviors. That is probably why the apostle Paul said he ended up doing what he didn't want to do, and didn't do what he wanted to! (See Rom. 7:15.) Perhaps if he would have understood the role of repressed memories on present behavior, he wouldn't have been so frustrated and could have more effectively worked with God to overcome that weakness.

(Nancy) It was the Sunday after Thanksgiving, and I was in the beginning stages of baking the gingerbread cookies that was my custom to do for the children of our church. I had rolled out the dough and was about to place the first sheets of formed "gingerbread men" into the oven when Ron entered the kitchen. I should have known by the look on his face that there was about to be an explosion. "I suppose these cookies are for someone else, as usual. Are you planning any for us at all?" he asked disgustedly.

I held my breath. What should I answer? No matter what I would say, I would be wrong. Finally the words just spewed from my mouth without forethought. "How long will you make me suffer during the holidays for what your parents did to you in childhood?"

He gave no answer, but I could tell that he was not happy! He turned on his heels and retreated to the safety of his study and his computer. I continued my baking project.

Two hours later, Ron came back to the kitchen. "Honey," he said, "You will never again suffer a miserable holiday. You're right; I have been making you pay for what my mother did to me, and that's not fair. Just because Christmas was hell in childhood is no excuse for me to recreate that for you and the kids. I've made my decision. After Christmas when decorations are 75 percent off, we'll buy the finest tree we can find, and you can decorate it however you'd like. I am choosing to enjoy the holidays with you and the family from now on!"

What a shock! And what a blessing! Ron even bought a little train, like the one that had been taken away from him one childhood Christmas, to place around the base of our new tree. He did the work necessary to care for the feelings from the past, and in so doing, created joy in the present and for the future.

Throughout the generations humanity has sought the reasons for behaviors, unable to recognize that most of our decisions are made as we look through the emotional filter of our past experiences. This filter stands between the past and the present, and its content substantially influences our choices. When the filter gets clogged with debris (painful memories and negative emotions), it causes malfunction. It is only as the filter is cleaned that we can see the truth of the present without distortion, that we can make logical decisions, minus layers of old pain. It is only as we remove the infection from the wound that we can hope to heal it. This is the process known in spiritual terms as *sanctification*.

CHAPTER 5

When You Don't Feel Loved and Nobody Cares

"The greatest terror a child can have is that he is not loved, and rejection is the hell he fears."
John Joseph Evoy

Everyone has felt the stab of rejection. Maybe you were just a kid when your dad left home or your mom suffered depression. Maybe it was when your first love ended up dating your best friend. Maybe it was when the baseball captain chose you last. Maybe you felt that stab when your wife didn't like the negligee you gave her for your anniversary. Or when your husband said "Yuk!" as he tasted your gourmet casserole. Are you the one who never gets an invitation to the party? Do you feel you don't belong and no one really cares? Or maybe you just feel that you don't need people; you're a loner, and you like it that way. If so, it is quite likely that you are the victim of rejection.

Webster defines rejection as "refusal to accept, receive, hear or consider important." Rejection is a self-defeating feeling of hopelessness that comes from damages occurring during prenatal and early childhood years. When the child's needs are not met, the child feels that he or she isn't important and, therefore, isn't worth much. Experiences in later years compound the damage done when character is being forged in early childhood.

John Joseph Evoy, a clinical psychologist in his classic book *The Rejected: Psychological Consequences of Parental*

Rejection, states that "rejection is a reported subjective experience. As such, it is not capable of exact definition nor of an operational definition. . . . As clients *described* the phenomenon of rejection, what was it? It was *their emotionally toned knowledge that they were not loved and wanted—for themselves—by one or both parents.*

Evoy makes the point that children do not question whether or not their parents treat them correctly. They merely assume that their parents were always right in their attitude and evaluation of the child. Even though the child may dislike, resent, or be hurt by the parent, they still feel both emotionally and cognitively that their parents are correct. They see them as omniscient and omnipotent giants; they see them as gods.

"Rejection," Evoy continues, "was not something these individuals happened to feel when they were depressed or otherwise out of sorts and which later disappeared when their spirits picked up. Rather, once they openly came to recognize the very painful feeling that they were rejected, it remained constant for them. Even when they happened not to be aware of it, the feeling of rejection did not go away. . . . Even successful psychotherapy did not phase out the hurt flowing from the experiences of rejection. It did, however, help the rejected to understand their rejection and cope more effectively with it" (15). This is another way of saying "The truth will set you free!"

Research has confirmed that feelings of rejection can begin within a child at five and a half months gestation, when the unborn child begins to respond emotionally to the feelings of the mother. (See chapter 2.) If the baby is unplanned, conceived at an inconvenient time, or is just not wanted, the unborn child interprets mother's feelings about the baby as rejection. This is also true if the male figure in the home is abusive to the pregnant mother. Because mother and baby are linked by a cord of life, the unborn child perceives that the rejection mother receives is really directed toward the baby. As a result, the mother's rejection becomes that baby's rejection.

Often children who are adopted feel rejected by their birth parents, even though they are loved and adored by their adoptive parents. The child retains an empty place where their birth parents should be and will always wonder, "Why did they give me away? What was it about me that they couldn't accept?" Usually that is the question that must be answered by the birth mother when in adult years the child searches for and finds her.

When a child expresses feelings and words that are discounted, laughed at, or condemned as dumb or stupid, the child feels rejected. Rejection can also be caused by loving parents who become too busy or preoccupied to meet the child's need for attention and approval. The parent who is overprotective, preventing the child from experiencing age-appropriate activities or playing with other children, inadvertently promotes feelings of rejection within the child. Even a parental look of disappointment can be interpreted by the sensitive child as rejection. "I did it wrong, therefore I am worthless." And *worthless* is exactly what Satan wants us to feel because worthlessness promotes hopelessness, and hopelessness produces emotional and spiritual death.

An integral part of Satan's deceptive scheme is to convince humankind of the lie that our behavior determines our value. The lie is repeatedly reinforced each time our behavior is beneath the standard of excellence set by self or others or each time we feel rejected by another. Feelings of rejection can be stimulated just by finding ourselves in circumstances similar to a previous incident when we felt rejected. Daily, feelings of rejection surface to recondemn and devaluate. For some people these feelings of rejection may flood over them many times an hour.

Having been damaged, rejection becomes the foundation of the child's belief system, which is pretty well established by eight years of age. Doomed for life to see the world through rejection glasses, and to find rejection under every rock, these individuals go from day-to-day, in the ordinary course of life, being reinflicted with Satan's original damage. These feelings rob their joy, diminish their intellect, and sabotage their success.

Children perceive parental treatment differently. Some survive abuse with seemingly little effect while others are devastated by it. The impact of parents on their children's emotional and spiritual health is an accepted fact. But that's not the whole story. It is not only the parental treatment but the temperament of the child that determines the outcome. A child's mind print will color the view of every circumstance of life. Some children can easily forget an injustice, while others cannot recover from unreasonable treatment.

It's during the earliest years that the strongest impressions are made. Even before children have language to express their pain or logic to excuse it away, the memories filed in the subconscious mind can end up driving their thoughts, feelings, and behaviors for a lifetime. (See chapter 4.) Repeated acts in a given course become habits—and habits are hard to break. They may be modified in later years by conscientious training using behavior modification techniques, but they are seldom changed completely.

But note: Behavior modification merely changes behavior, not necessarily the feelings and thoughts that result from early damage. Feelings and thoughts can only be changed through the process of looking at the past, processing through the pain, and counting on God to bring "beauty out of ashes" as He has promised. (See Isa. 61: 3.) Too many apply behavior modification and think that the operation is complete. But recovery is a daily choice; a renewing of the mind.

God has designed that there are certain tasks to be accomplished early in the development of the human body and mind, with specific time frames allotted for each. Bonding with parents takes place in the first two to four hours of life. If during those critical hours parents are unavailable to hold and caress, to express tender words and show love and acceptance through smiles and looks of endearment, the baby is deprived of the experience necessary to bond with parents in the way God originally designed.

A newborn has perfect vision during those first few hours but can only focus for approximately 18 inches, which is almost the exact distance from where the baby is held in father's arms to his eyes. Picture the newborn who is whisked from delivery to an Isolette to save its life and kept within that tiny space for days and weeks at a time. What happens to the child who is denied the bonding experience, which is the foundation for the child's feelings of acceptance?

(Nancy) This was the experience of our little Naomi. Now add to the picture the hostile environment of our family at the time of her birth, and you can quickly realize the depth of the pain she must have felt. My health dictated that if we were to have a second child, her conception and birth must take place at a most inconvenient time for Ron and me.

Ron was in school full time and also ran a business of his own that required long hours of hard labor. We already had a fourteen-month-old daughter, and Ron was not happy about the thought of an added financial load. The stress in his life—the demand of late hours and heavy studies—was all-consuming. Yet my advanced state of endometriosis required a pregnancy then or never. Being an only child myself and knowing the loneliness I experienced, I had vowed to never have an only child. I would do whatever it would take, even at the loss of my own life, to create a sibling for our Sara. So reluctantly Ron participated in Naomi's conception, thinking that I would have held it against him for the rest of his life if he didn't. His own issues of rejection were so strong that he couldn't face the possibility of rejection from me.

I was critically ill during this pregnancy, and the pressure was too much for Ron. At the beginning of the seventh month, Ron left the house one morning for work. But by ten o'clock, I discovered he had never made it to work, and no one knew where he was. We had parted that morning on friendly terms with the usually perfunctory hug and kiss, but somehow my heart knew, when we couldn't find him, that he was gone. I paced the floor that day, gasping for a breath, carrying little Sara on my hip. My anxiety spilled over to her, and she could not rest. I cried until I had no tears left. I shared the trauma with no one, for fear of the repercussions Ron might suffer if he should return. At ten that night I called one of his professors who, with his wife, had taken our little family under his wing and loved us very dearly. He assured me that Ron would return. He and his wife offered to come to our home to be supportive, but I refused, saying that Ron would be embarrassed if he returned and found his professor at the house.

After our telephone prayer, Sara fell asleep in my arms, and I took her with me to our bed, where I fitfully dozed. At midnight the phone rang. I raced to the study to answer it and heard Ron's voice on the other end. He told me that he was already in Canada on his first stop to Europe. Innocently I asked him, "When are you coming home?" (Please understand that the sweetness of my voice was God's intervening.)

There was a long hesitation, and he said, "Tomorrow morning. Meet me at the airport."

I said, "I'll see you in the morning, Sweetheart. I love you," and hung up the phone.

I wrestled with my plight. "How would I get to the airport?" I asked myself. "He has the car." I decided I would have to borrow an old friend's SAAB. I would tell her Ron was stuck in Boston. "But I have no money, and what if the car needed gas?" I decided to ask my friend to fill the gas tank and that I would repay her when Ron got home.

Early in the morning, I primped as best I could, feeling like an overgrown watermelon, and dressed Sara in her ruffled dress. I got to Boston, but I had forgotten about the tunnel where there was a toll gate. I had to pay a dime to get through, and I had no money. I promised the guard to pay him double on my return, and amused by my dilemma, he let me go through.

As Ron got off the plane, I raced to him. We stood holding each other, both of us weeping and wondering "Why? Why? How would we ever find the answers? How could we continue?" We maintained our relationship the way many couples do, by sweeping the hurt under the rug, not looking at it or discussing it again for many years.

And so Naomi came into this world and into a family who was already on emotional overload. But it didn't end there. Satan refused to be defeated. As I approached the end of my eighth month, a local physician and family friend made a house call, and when he realized my precarious condition, he immediately called my obstetrician in Boston who was a Harvard medical professor specializing in difficult pregnancies. They prescribed a powerful diuretic, and a few days later I went for my regular prenatal exam. Dr. Gauld feared that the way things were going, I could not maintain the pregnancy without the sacrifice of my life. Yet, if I were to undergo anesthesia for a caesarian section, he feared I would die on the table because of my lung condition. So he sent me home to try an old method of stimulating the onset of labor.

It worked, and three hours later I was in full labor. Ron was with me during labor, but reluctantly, because he had "work" to do to support this growing family and was restless to get back to the job he had left.

Finally I sent him out of the room for a cold drink, called a nurse, and told her I needed the doctor immediately because something was wrong. The doctor came, and I begged him for an epidural to endure the pain. It was the only relief available, being minimally dilated.

Dr. Gauld was a grandfatherly type and stood talking to me with his hand on my abdomen for what seemed like an eternity, but he was timing the length of my contractions. Finally he said, "All right, girl, we are going to do this thing," and pushed the bed himself into delivery. Positioned on my side for the anesthesia, the team prepared my back for the epidural, and the nurse kept repeating, "Still contracting, Doctor. Still contracting, Doctor." I was in deepest agony! What I didn't know was that the placenta was tearing from the wall of the uterus, causing a prolonged contraction. In fifteen minutes when I was allowed to turn on my back, I was fully dilated. Then with two pushes Naomi was born. But the damage was already done, and Naomi was rushed immediately from delivery to preemie intensive care because of respiratory difficulties. I had heard no baby cries, but those within my mind drowned out the dread of an impending loss. Where was Ron?

Naomi was born blue from aspirating my blood during a placenta abruptia delivery. We were initially told that she had a fatal lung disease, but later the diagnosis was changed to aspiration pneumonia. It was almost a week before the physicians gave us any hope that she might live. We were not allowed to even see her until the end of her third day, and then I had to beg to just look at her. One of the nurses took pity on me and took her from the isolette allowing me to hold her for a few minutes. And then we had to leave her behind in the hospital for another ten days and were not allowed to visit.

It was a pretty rocky beginning for a little one who desperately needed to know she was really wanted and accepted. When we were given permission to finally bring her home, Ron refused to hold her. He immediately felt a dislike—a fear of her. It took him a few weeks to realize the reason for his feelings—she looked just like his mother, who had rejected him while he was still in utero.

Then to add another destructive ingredient to Naomi's already full compliment of rejection, I had to go to the hospital for surgery when she was three months of age. She had become so chubby and adorable I even called her my little "chubba-cheeks." I hated to leave her and her sister while I had this operation, but the doctors said it was imperative to have it done then.

My mother, a super nurse, came to our home to care for Naomi and Sara while I was away. Both the girls received abundant affection and care, but Naomi became ill the day I left. Repeated phone calls to the doctor, medications and instructions, which were followed to the letter, did not change the course of her sickness. Still she continued to lose weight, and by the day before I was to come home from the hospital, my mother feared that she was going to die. She walked the floor hugging, singing hymns to her, and asking the Lord to intervene.

The afternoon, when I returned home and saw her, remains vivid in my mind and strikes to the heart of my emotion even as I recall it today. She was so thin, so pale, and so gaunt. I held her close to me and cried, yet I was afraid to show too much emotion for fear of hurting my mother's feelings. Immediately I went to the phone and called our pediatrician. In tears, I told him of Naomi's condition and pleading for his intervention. He was kind and sympathetic and advised that we bring her and my suitcase to the hospital, saying that if she needed to be admitted, he would admit me too.

In the car on the way to the hospital, I clung to her and kissed her emaciated little cheeks over and over again, crying and pleading with God to save her. In the examining room, Dr. Holden looked at her dehydrated little body and was obviously concerned. "Before I admit her," he said, "sit in this rocking chair, Nancy, and see if she will take this bottle of pedialyte (a formula of electrolytes) for you." Mother had been offering the same thing to her for days but with no success.

I held her closely in the manner to which she had become accustomed in those three months we had been together, and I offered her the nipple. With the minimal strength she had left, she looked into my eyes and slowly opened her mouth. Ever so gently she sucked at the liquid, and we patiently waited until she had consumed all four ounces. It was a miracle!

"Well, Nancy, you can take her home," the doctor advised. "She is over the hump now that you are home. I think that she was missing you so much that her little body had just shut down. She now has what she needs to live."

It still blows my mind as I write of it today—that one week without a mother can have such a devastating effect on a baby. Perhaps if she had not experienced the earlier rejections, she would not have felt so rejected by my week-long absence.

Naomi received the damage of rejection while she was still in the womb, and it played itself out every day of her growing years. She hated to have her picture taken, whether alone or in the family group. Her tendency was to hide behind her older sister, to push Sara out into the limelight while she remained in the shadows. These were unconscious ways of saying, "I don't belong to this family."

At age thirteen, having begun his own recovery, her daddy took her on a date and told her the truth, that he had indeed rejected her during those early years. He assured her that it was not because of something wrong with her but from his own pain. His inability to show acceptance had come from the fact that he had never experienced it himself as a child. One must possess before one can give away. He also told her the truth—that he had not loved her but that it was not about her. It was about his inability to love. He had never been taught to love, but he assured her he was learning.

Holding her hand across the table, he committed to her that from that moment on he would do all in his power to prove his love and acceptance of her. "I will love you with no strings attached. I will not withhold my love or make you perform for me to receive my love. I am committing to you this day that there is not one thing you can do to ever make me stop loving you."

They have grown in their love for each other since then, and in Naomi's thinking, her relationship with her dad is perfect. It is only miles that separate them now.

Rejection, however, does not always occur as a result of a dysfunctional family. Sometimes it is purely accidental. For example, let's say a toddler is suddenly frightened by the thunder crashing outside and desperately needs comfort and reassurance from his parents. But at the same time, daddy is out in the garage, and just as mother is about to pick up the child, she hears her husband frantically calling for her to help him. What should she do? She says to the older child, "Take care of Johnny, Daddy needs me," as if the baby doesn't need her. The result can be an emotional wound that could develop into a sense of rejection, especially if that scenario happens repeatedly. "Someone is always more important than I am," is the message the child receives. And each time this happens, it's as if the wound becomes re-infected with the germ of rejection, and with each exposure the wound becomes harder to heal.

The average mother or father would say, "But we couldn't help that. It wasn't intentional." But intent or motive doesn't matter to children, because they lack the ability to reason from cause to effect and to take into consideration the motives for certain actions. Children respond emotionally, not logically.

Regardless of motive, the damage is still a damage. Children are often injured by a scrape or cut incurred in an accidental fall. The damage is real. If you neglect the wound, it will fester and eventually develop a systemic infection, which is life-threatening. Parents intend to protect their children from danger and injury. They put safety plugs into the electrical outlets, they install safety catches on their cupboard doors, and safety gates on the stairways. But in this world, controlled by Satan, accidents still happen. But just because an accident isn't intentional, does that mean you ignore the physical injury? Of course not!

So it is with emotional accidents in childhood. Children get injured. Most of the time these injuries are unintentional. However, the damage is real, and the wound must be cleaned and disinfected, or the harmful emotional infection we term "rejection" will intensify.

We are given first-aid classes on how to care for physical wounds, but we need the same for psychological wounds. Just as a physical infection poisons the body, so does emotional trauma poison the mind, affecting a child's thoughts, feelings, and behaviors—and the pain continues into adulthood or until the person seeks emotional healing.

Jason was only fifteen months of age when his brother was born into the family, usurping his favored-son position. Three months later his parents had an opportunity to spend two weeks in Europe. They knew about the classic research done by John Bowlby on the importance of bonding in early childhood and how absence of the parents during this critical period could cause intense feelings of rejection, and they didn't want that to happen to their children. So they made plans to leave their children with close relatives: Jason would stay with his aunt who had a son Jason's age—and who adored Jason. Jeremy would stay with Grandma and Grandpa.

All went well for Jeremy. He was the center of his grand-parents' attention. But those two weeks were a nightmare for Jason. Although Jason and his cousin had previously enjoyed playing together, now without Jason's mother, Jason needed comfort from his aunt. But the moment his aunt picked him up, her son got intensely jealous and demanded attention. Instead of playing the two weeks away, Jason's cousin spent the time hitting him, pushing him, and biting him. Each time it happened, the aunt would pick Jason up—which only fueled her own son's jealousy.

If someone would have reported what was going on back home, Mom and Dad would have canceled their plans and returned home immediately. But no one said anything until they returned two weeks later, and the damage had already been done.

Decisions parents make must always be child-centered; they must be child-friendly. But sometimes, regardless of the information parents have, accidents happen. And when they do, you need an emotional first-aid kit.

The first aid you need to render is acceptance. You do this by doing exactly what you would do if your child had a physical injury.

First, you hold the child close. It's your closeness that gives the child the reassurance of their security in your presence. In the holding close you assess the damage.

Second, you speak comforting words to the child. Use your rocking-chair voice and speak words of affirmation and assurance. "You'll be OK, Sweetheart. Mommy loves you. We'll fix it."

Third, you affirm that the injury has indeed happened.

Believe your child. The details may not be clear or totally accurate, but if the child *feels* injured, the child *is* injured. You affirm that the injury has happened by verbalizing the emotional pain that you perceive your child has experienced. "You were scared when Mommy left you, weren't you?" Or "Mommy feels sad that you were hurt."

Fourth, if the child is old enough, encourage the child to talk about what happened. Listen not only to the details as the child perceives them but also to the child's body language and evidences of emotion. The more the child speaks about it, defusing the pent-up emotions, the more likely that healing will occur. And being able to confide in one's parents creates a safe place where future rejection or emotional traumas can be shared. Considering that parents stand in the place of God to their children, this listening teaches a lesson that God also listens and cares.

Fifth, assure the child that his or her welfare is your primary concern. You will protect the child from further damage and do whatever is necessary to heal the wound, regardless of whether the injury happened inside the family or from others.

Sixth, take active steps to prevent further injuries. If there is someone who has inflicted pain upon your child, you must take whatever action is necessary so it never happens again. Your acceptance of the child is demonstrated by your willingness to protect your child from further injury. When you take this action, children sense that they are important to you and, therefore, have personal value.

Seventh, pray a hedge of protection around your child and pray for the wisdom to successfully resolve the damage. Your prayers are God's permission to attack Satan's forces and destroy his control of your children's emotional well-being. By calling on God to intervene, you are a model for your children, teaching them faith in God's power to overcome the damaging effects of rejection on your children's thoughts, feelings, and behaviors, which could prevent them from becoming emotionally mature individuals. Parents must say, as did the father of a deaf son 2,000 years ago, "Lord I believe, help thou my unbelief" (Mark 9:24). We may not see immediate results, but they will be as sure as tomorrow's sunrise.

Satan would have us as parents carry the guilt, but that only exacerbates the problem. While unhealed feelings of rejection will ultimately destroy a child, so do feelings of guilt destroy parents.

Satan's master plan is that people will reject each other, thus Satan employs humans to do his dirty work. God's acceptance of us is like an insurance policy; not against further damage but reassuring us that regardless of the damage, He can repair it. In addition, God's Word details our part in the recovery process. (See chapter 11.)

Our part is to take God at His Word and steadfastly cling to His promises for the salvation of our children. "Fear not for I am with you; I will bring your offspring from the east [where they are dispersed] and gather you from the west. I will say to the north, Give up! and to the south, Keep not back. Bring my sons from afar and my daughters from the ends of the earth—Even everyone who is called by My name, whom I have created for My glory, whom I have formed, whom I have made" (Isa. 43:5-7, The Amplified Bible).

Perhaps you are concerned about yourself and the rejection from which you suffer. This is what God says, "I have chosen you and have not rejected you. So do not fear, for I am with you; do not be dismayed, for I am your God. I will strengthen you and help you; I will uphold you with my righteous right hand" (Isa. 41:9, 10, NIV).

Regardless of the depth of pain you may feel, the despair over lost relationships and an inability to feel accepted by earthly parents or your Heavenly Father, God offers you HOPE and a path toward recovery to follow. His love is constant and unconditional. He offers to carry the burden of rejection you carry. Aren't you tired of the load?

CHAPTER 6

The Beginnings of Our Resentments

"I have chosen you and have not rejected you.
So do not fear for I am with you;
do not be dismayed, for I am your God.
Isaiah 41:9, NIV

Rejection is not a one-time event. It is an intense and often repeated feeling of worthlessness that shows itself on the playground when a child says, "Nobody wants to play with me," and in teenage years, "How come no one asks me on a date?" In marriage it rears its ugly head when we assume that our partner does not accept us as we need to be accepted. It shows up when we make value judgments, "If she really loved me, supper would be on the table every night when I get home." "If he really loved me, he would talk to me, not about people, places, and things, but about what he thinks and how he feels. He would dream with me and plan." "Why is it I feel that someday he will leave me for the princess in the long white gown?" "Why is it I fear that she will abandon me for some knight in shining armor?"

We asked these questions too.

(Ron) Yes, I've been there! I was the "Butch" my sister Phyllis spoke of when she said, "Nobody wanted Butch." My birth was unplanned, and I was unwanted. Phyllis remembers the day I was brought home from the hospital and laid in my crib, even though she was only eight years old at the time. She remembers that I wasn't picked up again, despite my cries for food, cleanliness, or cuddling, until she put down her dollies and picked me up. Mother must have been sick. She must have had a severe case of post-partum psychosis to have neglected me so.

My three older siblings were breast fed; I didn't get that benefit. They had their physical needs met; mine were not. My mother was a child herself and just couldn't cope. And Father was no help. During the first eighteen months when the development of trust is the emotional task to be completed, there was no adult I could trust.

In fact, I vividly recall the harsh, inhumane punishment inflicted on my older brother George. I have no idea what he kept doing to warrant the severe razor strap beatings that Dad frequently gave him. I remember him screaming for Dad to stop hitting and the sight of my mother sitting on the cellar steps egging my father on to harsher and lengthier beatings. I wondered then, "Why would she betray her own son?" Many times George would come to bed screaming in pain and sob half the night. If my parents could do this to my older brother, what were they planning for me?

The interesting thing is, while George was abusively touched, I was *never* touched. Every waking moment I felt the rejection. Even though I burned down the garage at age five and was considered the neighborhood hellion, I never got any attention. When bad behavior didn't work, I tried going straight. I went through all the levels of scouting and became an Eagle Scout. Yet the night of the award ceremony, the troop leader had to call a volunteer out of the audience to stand in for my father—and we lived only two blocks away.

Vividly I remember being about six and finding a quarter in the gutter as I walked home from school. My first thought was to race to the candy store for my favorite— Tootsie Rolls. The size that could be purchased then for a nickel probably isn't even made now. They were huge! I marched into the house clutching those five tootsie rolls, like a knight in shining armor coming home from battle with the spoils. *Mother will be so proud. Maybe I can share one with her*, I thought.

But my reception clearly sent that idea out the window! She spotted the Tootsie Rolls the moment I came through the door. "And where did you get the candy, young man?" she demanded, hands on her hips and suspicion in her eye. Of course, I told her how I had found the quarter and then had taken it to the store to buy the candy. She was angry! "You take those Tootsie Rolls back to the store and get that quarter back. Then go from door to door in the neighborhood and find the person who lost the money. Make sure that you return the quarter to that person," she shouted. I had told the truth and instead of being rewarded, I ended up being humiliated.

Even in my childish mind, I felt the injustice of it. But I complied with her demand, hoping to receive a warmer reception when I returned home empty-handed. I remember standing at the candy counter and having to return those precious Tootsie Rolls, as if I had been a criminal who had stolen them from the store. And who would say they had not lost the quarter when I was asking to return it to someone?

The picture of how things worked at home was becoming clearer. If you tell the truth, you are accused of lying and are punished. So I learned to lie, hoping to avoid punishment.

Grandpa Miller was the only adult in my family who connected with me in any way. He really loved me. He taught me to tie my shoes, he let me hang from the rope as he rang the church bells every Sunday, and he planted a garden with me. Then came the day I was handed a quarter and told to go to the movies. It was not a reward; it was a bribe to get me out of the house. When I returned, the house was filled with people, weeping and drinking coffee. But Grandpa wasn't there. I never saw him again. There was no explanation as to his disappearance.

It seemed like every time I was given a quarter and sent to the movies something precious was snatched from me in my absence. For example, the Saturday I came home to find a large truck in our driveway with men carrying out our furniture. I was then told that we were moving. But what about my garden? Would I never see the flowers bloom that Grandpa helped me plant? Would Grandpa ever see them? Another time my black lab disappeared, and then my cat and all her kittens were gone. It was years later that I learned my folks had put my dog to sleep and drowned the cat and her kittens while I was at the movies. Why is it always my possessions, my treasures, that are disappearing? What is it about me?

I remember the time I just wanted to give Ma some apples, hoping that she would bake a pie and let me at least have a taste. I went to the neighbor lady who owned an orchard and asked if I could pick up the drops. She hollered at me, "No, you can't. Get off my property." My need for parental acceptance was greater than her threat, so I climbed the fence and picked up a sack full of drops. Ma was thrilled. But moments later the police arrived with the lady who owned the orchard. She pointed at me and said, "That's the boy who picked my apples." I tried to explain, but no one would listen. As she was leaving she called over her shoulder, "I would have given them to you, if you had just asked." I couldn't believe she had lied so blatantly! The rule was reinforced in my head, "If you lie they'll believe you; if you tell the truth, they won't."

Rejection, from experiences like the above, became the driving force of my life. Ultimate rejection by my father came the night he died in my arms. I had just turned sixteen. It was Halloween night, and Dad had been out having fun scaring the neighborhood kids. For once I was in bed early, when Ma raced up the stairs screaming hysterically, "Come quick, your dad is dying. The minute I saw my dad's ashen gray complexion, I called for the ambulance and began mouth-to-mouth resuscitation and continued it for what seemed like an eternity. But it was too late.

As my dad lay lifeless in my arms, it occurred to me, He had to be dead for me to get close to him. I thought however, that I was to blame. Being told all my life that I messed up everything I touched, I figured that in a way, I had killed my dad because my CPR skills were inadequate; I must not have done it right.

The next morning, believe it or not, a neighbor lady gave me a dollar bill and told me to go to the movies. On the way there I bought a paper just to read the obituaries. In my secret hiding place under the bridge, I read my father's name. The stark reality of this loss hit me with a crushing blow. I now felt his ultimate rejection. "I must be so worthless that Dad had to die to leave me," I thought. Hope of ever building a relationship with my father was gone. I screamed to God, "If you are really there, I want to make a deal with you. Take my dad to heaven and I'll take his place in hell." All my life I had done everything to get my dad's approval, and now at his death I was even willing to give up my own salvation to gain it.

It was only recently, in contemplating my father's love for me, that I have realized that my worth and my ability to relax and feel comfortable about who I am is related to the one positive memory I have of my dad—letting me drive. As a toddler I recall that twice my dad put me on his lap while driving the family car so I could make believe that I was

driving. Then one night when I was fifteen, my father allowed me to drive the family car home from work. It occurred only once. As I think of it now, I realize that those
were the only times I was close to my dad.

Today, there isn't anything I like better than getting behind the wheel and driving for long periods of time. Somehow, it gives me a sense of who I am. Behind the wheel I feel
relaxed, comforted, secure, and capable. It was in the driver's
seat where I found the parental acceptance and warmth I
had craved.

(Nancy) The rejection in my story is not as overt as Ron's.
It was more perceived on my part than actual, and yet the
pain of my rejection was intense.

At first glance if you looked at my loving, Christian family and realized how much they loved me, you would have
never believed that I could be emotionally abused. Yet the
circumstances of my early years set me up to feel rejection.
How would it be possible for an only child of a strong Christian home to feel rejected? Could these feelings be only her
imagination run wild, or were her perceptions colored somehow?

Two weeks after Mother and Dad's wedding, my father
was drafted into the army. World War II had begun, and his
term of duty demanded overseas service for most of the first
four years of my life. I had been conceived while Dad was on
leave after boot camp and was born while he was in medic
training here in the states. My baby brother, conceived during the time we spent with my father while he was taking
advanced medic training, was born six months after he left
America for the front lines of battle in Europe. Ten days
later my brother died because of a hospital accident, leaving me an only child.

My mother became critically ill from infectious hepatitis and was emotionally depleted as well, spending a good portion of that next year in bed. Fortunately, Mother and I were living with her parents, so there was someone to care for both of us.

Grandma and Grandpa were extremely gentle and overly permissive. They were from northern England, where no one is a stranger. I can still hear Grandma's words as she wiped away my tears. "Cumoosh, Luv." (Translated: "Come, hush, Love.") She would pull me on her lap in the creaky rocker, and I'd lay my head on her ample bosom. She would pat me and say, "Comoosh, Luv," and there I'd fall into a peaceful sleep.

When the war was over, a man I didn't know showed up at the back door with a dress uniform and a candy bar in every pocket. He was hoping to entice me to come to him— but the real truth was, he was looking for acceptance. I had seen his picture and been repeatedly instructed to call him "Daddy." So when I saw him I used the correct word but did not comprehend its full meaning, for Daddy was a stranger to me. The truth was, I called every stranger in uniform "Daddy."

My father's parents lived in the next town. Dad's father was a powerful athlete but a very quiet man who did not share his thoughts or feelings. His mother was a tiny woman with large demands. She forced strict obedience upon my father but had no tender relationship with him. Dad's parents disowned him when he became an Adventist, and they wouldn't even come to his wedding. So my father felt the pain of rejection as a child and repeatedly as an adult from his family of origin. In addition to their rejection of Dad, these grandparents did not see me until, when pregnant with my brother, my mom took a bus and then climbed a

steep hill in a blizzard in an attempt to force them to acknowledge us. At that time, my father was on the front lines
as a medic in the thick of German territory. Mother chided
them for not having seen us since before her marriage to
Dad and forced them to return home with her to meet me.

How can a dad who is so filled with rejection pour out
acceptance on a little girl who needed it so desperately?
When he returned from war, Dad took his rightful place in
the home, not knowing that he would have to prove his love
and acceptance of me before he could move from being a
father to being my dad. Unfortunately, he came on like
gangbusters, dutifully carrying out the role he felt was his.
What he did not know was that the little girl he was
parenting was even more sensitive than he, and I lived in
fear of him.

Within two days Dad had found an apartment for our
little family, and I was taken away from my loving grandparents with their constant words of adoration and acceptance. Father needed my allegiance and loyalty and longed
to be included in my life. My love, however, was not coaxed
and wooed from me; it was required.

Dad had never felt love and acceptance in his childhood
home, so he had no idea of how to give me what I needed.
He was desperately needy himself for the acceptance he
would never receive from his parents. When he was eight or
nine he got the first of many jobs and faithfully gave his
check to his mother, intrusting her to take out some for his
room and board and put the rest in a fund so he could someday fulfill his dream to attend the Julliard Conservatory of
Music and become a concert pianist. Two weeks before he
was to graduate from high school, he asked his mother for
the money. "It's gone!" she said, "I used it."

Dad was devastated. In addition to the rejection he had felt throughout his childhood, his mother had just destroyed his lifelong dream. He immediately packed his few belongings and left home, not bothering to finish high school.

His father died while he was fighting overseas, so when he returned home, his feelings of his own personal rejection re-surfaced. Then not long after the war, he was rejected again by his mother when he refused to become involved in a real estate venture that would have been a financial handicap for him. His mother never forgave him for that. Eight years later she had a massive stroke, was paralyzed, and unable to speak.

Grandma refused to stay in our home or even in the home of her only daughter, which would have cost very little. Instead, she lived out her existence for an additional nine years in a local nursing home. All her properties had to be sold to pay the care bills and when her savings were exhausted, Dad paid for her care. Throughout the years he lovingly tended to his mother, visiting nearly every day on his way home from work. He was still searching for one glimmer of acceptance from her, but it was not forthcoming. The question is, Would he have recognized acceptance if she had given it?

One thing needs to be clearly understood in both Ron's history and mine. Would-be parents have great intentions; hoping to be the best parents in the world. What happens to foil their plans is that their own histories get in the way. The past colors their perceptions, damages their thoughts and feelings, and ends up creating behaviors that do not prove to be a blessing to their children. And so their own children get damaged in the wake of parental pain.

When Dad came back into our lives after the war, my

mother became the interpreter of Dad's behavior to me. Somehow she sensed that she needed to communicate to me what my father couldn't express about my worth and value. Strangely, he could share those words with my mother, but he couldn't tell me. Instead, he put all his expectations before me and demanded my compliance.

Caught in the undertow of Dad's past, I came to believe that my love and acceptance was based on my performance, so I became a good actress. I made believe that my performance was really who I was, when in truth it was what I thought *they* wanted. But I felt that I could never quite reach my father's expectations, regardless of how hard I tried. The truth is that my fear of him thwarted my ability to meet his expectations.

Fear paralyzes! And I was truly afraid of Dad. The only male figure I had known was my maternal grandpa, whom I called Pa. He was a pussy cat! His qualities were of the loving, tender, and undemanding type, and he played the part of a sibling more than an authoritarian adult. It was a puzzle for my child mind to understand the commanding military role my father played in the family when contrasted to the gentle friendship role my grandfather played.

In spite of not being able to go to Julliard, Dad was a concert pianist, and he expected I should be too. He tried for a year to teach me piano lessons, and the harder he tried, the more scared I became of him. He had little patience with me, and if I could not play something the way he thought I should, I would hear stinging words, or he would leave the room in utter disgust. Finally he gave up trying to teach me and searched within a fifty-mile radius to find a teacher worthy of his child. I bonded immediately with the grandmotherly Olive Roberts. But, unfortunately, I practiced at home, often with my father standing over me—and I never could get it right.

Here's a vivid memory; a perfect example of the psychological law that fear paralyzes. It was my first piano recital. My father was proudly perched on the edge of his seat in the second row, and it was my turn. I sat at the concert grand, and an incredible fear came over me. I could not remember the title of the piece I was to play, nor could I remember where it started or what key it was written in. I sat there on the bench and began to cry, feeling deeply humiliated and knowing that I was an embarrassment to Dad. My piano teacher whispered, "E. Honey, It's the key of E." But I was blank. After an eternity, I got up and went to my seat where I heard my father heave a big sigh behind me. Was it disgust or disappointment?

What I longed to hear from him just once was, "It's OK, Honey. It's OK! It's not that important." Maybe then my fear would have gone. But instead, on the way home he said, "What is the matter with you? Why can't you play like . . . ?" (He named a childhood chum.) Dad only meant to help me. He had no idea how his words hurt and no idea how to tell me that it was OK. I tried very, very hard to get his acceptance, but my efforts were just not good enough. At times I'm still tempted to feel disappointed in myself; disgusted that I cannot meet my father's expectations which have become my own.

What does childhood rejection look like as the child grows into adulthood? The most obvious manifestations are hostility, anxiety, depression, insecurity, feelings of inferiority, and feelings of inadequacy. Less obvious symptoms are inhibitions, indifference, quietness, and extreme submissiveness.

For many years when confronted with what looked like rejection to me, I would feel insecure and would *withdraw* into myself, uncertain of my real identity or worth. I would run to the privacy of my own mind where I thought my thoughts and felt my feelings quietly; alone.

Each person needs a foundation of consistent unconditional love and acceptance and parents who are trustworthy in order to build a safe structure that will contain and enable them to meet the rest of life's stresses successfully. It seemed to me that my foundation was securely in place. But when Dad returned from war, the truths I had come to believe were no longer true, and I found myself on shaky, sandy ground. I had thought I was OK, safe, secure, and valuable, but as I watched him, I came to realize that he was the capable one, and I could not possibly live up to his standards or compete with his talents. In comparison to him, I was *inferior*—a nothing.

Sucking my thumb while being curled up in the corner of the sofa was my method of confronting my *insecurity*, and I held on to this habit for dear life until I was sixteen. I hid this perception of inferiority somewhere deep inside, and for the world I acted the part they chose for me to play. My only confidant was my cocker spaniel, who frequently heard a monologue of my warped thoughts and feelings, occasional joys, and frequent sorrows. The dog was put to sleep when I was fourteen, but the thumb-sucking ceased only when I was preparing to enter college at age sixteen. I have learned that even the loss of a beloved pet can be interpreted by a child as rejection. This is especially true in early pubescence, when girls are enamored with the idea of love. Many find the acceptance and love of an animal to be very crucial to them, especially if they do not have a boyfriend. I was one of those who mourned deeply for my lost pet and felt once again the pain of rejection.

Rejection has many negative spinoffs. For example, *even though the world might applaud accomplishments, rejected children will feel inadequate and inferior until they hear and feel parental affirmation.*

I remember one occasion when I sang "I Believe" to a packed house of patients at the local state hospital with Dad accompanying me at the piano. Wow, what a response! They clapped and whistled and stood to their feet. I remember thinking that at least an auditorium of mental patients approved, and then rationalized that they had probably applauded for Dad, because he was a well-loved and admired employee there. I obviously suffered from feelings of inadequacy!

Depression manifested itself to me somewhat later in life—after I married Ron. When I realized that I was a disappointment to Ron as well as to Dad, the childhood pain surfaced once again. I responded to Ron the way I responded to my father, by *withdrawing*. Depression so ate away at the concept of myself that I started becoming physically ill shortly after we were married, and in the first seven years of our marriage while Ron was going through college, I had four major surgeries and two babies. I found myself hospitalized on several occasions for various life-threatening illnesses, mostly having to do with my heart. My face would break out with an oozing, itchy rash, which made me look horrible and served to create distance between my husband and me. The distance I felt from Ron was the distance I felt from my father.

The only way I knew to express the intense anger boiling inside me was to slam kitchen cupboard doors. So when Ron would leave our apartment for school or work, I would open all of the kitchen doors and with clenched teeth and loud mumbling, I would slam each door shut with as much vehemence as I could muster. It was the only way I knew to get out the *hostility* bottled inside me without hurting Ron or the children. As I reflect now, however, I see that those tantrums were frightening to my babies and must have made them feel insecure.

I assumed that my inadequacies were the cause of my rejection in our marriage. So to compensate, I *anxiously* overworked, trying to prove my worth and value. If I had sat down for a minute in my overcrowded day and would hear Ron coming up the stairs, I would quickly jump to my feet and get busy doing something. I had to appear super-human, superperfect, and totally without flaw!

I lived in constant exhaustion, thus in constant depression. I was sick all the time! While living in our first parsonage, a neighbor came to visit me while I was in the hospital's intensive care unit. Not being a Christian, she used crass words that struck home, "Go ahead, Nance, keep it up. Feed ninety people for breakfast. Let your house be Grand Central Station for all the church members. Sew for everybody, feed the world. Do, do, do, all the time, and you'll just keep getting sicker and sicker. And when you crack up or die, Ron can just go find some blonde to marry!" What a dose of stark reality!

Even though I worked myself ragged for Ron's acceptance, as well as the admiration of the "saints," the work was in vain. Ron controlled, and I cowered. He barked out the orders, and I did his bidding. He carried and controlled the money, and I worked nights so he would have enough to carry. He allowed $5 a week groceries, and I lay awake figuring how to make it stretch. He demanded undivided attention and constant availability to fill his needs, so I allowed him to put a pay phone in the parsonage where we lived so he could control my time and his money. I was as *submissive* as I could be, and all the while he verbally reinforced what I already "knew," that I would never be good enough to receive his acceptance.

As I think back I can only say, "It's incredible how *the past dominates the present.*" And what's so unbelievable is that I kept up this performance pace for almost twenty-eight years—long after I already had the approval I needed from Ron. The truth is, it had become a habit. It was very difficult for me to part with the lie I had believed for so long.

Anxieties took control over me, and I existed from one crisis to another. My daily routine revolved around my need to please Ron so that he would love me or to please the children so they would love me too. I told my thoughts and shared my pain with no one, including my husband. When I tried to share with him, somehow I always came out looking like a real jerk—a case for the local mental institution. I learned to be *quiet* and to hide my emotions as well as the truth of my pain.

I was desperately lonely but had to be guarded about the time I spent talking with neighbors because Ron was threatened by every contact I had with someone other than him. I made every effort possible to guard the secret agony of our marriage, so that he would always look good to the parishioners and family, but I paid a high price for the secrecy. The more truth I hid, the more serious my illnesses became. My life as an actress had to end.

Parents stand in the place of God to their children. They comprehend God by watching the attributes and behaviors of the parents. Children assume that if they can't see the parents, the parents do not exist, nor does God exist, because He cannot be seen either. So how is a child to form a healthy concept of God with a missing or rejecting father and/or mother? Is it possible to picture God as loving, accepting, and always available under such conditions?

I could only see who God was by looking at my dad, who was first absent and then harsh. And the truth is that the same fear I had of my father was transferred to God. Fortunately, the influence of Mother was soft, gentle, and loving, and that helped in my interpretation of God's character. There did come a time in those first few years after Dad returned from war that I saw God (Mother) as having divided loyalties, leaving or betraying me at important times. I now assume that this perception came from the dramatic atmosphere change and the amount of attention I lost when he arrived. Her changes were understandable, given the fact that they had lost so many precious days, weeks, and months of their new marriage to the horror of the war. Unfortunately, young children do not have the capacity to reason thus.

Years later I learned that to fear God means to adore Him with a tender feeling, not to be afraid of Him. But how can you adore someone to whom you are not bonded? Dad had been missing during those first few important bonding hours and days of my life. He came home when he could, yet his brief visits were too short to accomplish the building of a relationship with him. As a result, we both lost out as we carried the pain of not really connecting positively with each other. We were kind; we were courteous. But we were not connected.

While my dad was loving and tender with other children and adults, giving them space to make mistakes and recover from them, he somehow expected me to be perfect all the time. Perhaps it was because he thought of me as an extension of himself, and he demanded perfection of himself. So I would receive the chiding he would quietly give himself. I understand now that his proud and arrogant behaviors were only coverups for his bleeding, rejected heart.

My childish perception of God was that He was watching from the great white throne waiting for me to make mistakes, just the way Dad watched and always caught me doing something wrong. What a joy to be finally freed from that lie!

(Ron) I reacted to my rejection with absolute rage. Even as a child I was *hostile* and *aggressive*, expressing my rage in overt ways. I burned down my family's garage at age five, was always taking some mechanical or electrical thing apart just to see if I could put it back together again successfully, and would make flaming arrows and shoot them into the sides of passing semitrucks. With my buddies, I would play cops and robbers or cowboys and Indians in a stone quarry with real guns and live ammunition. The bullets would fly about my head and ricochet off the stone walls. The more dangerous the activity, the more thrilling it was to me.

I *sabotaged school success* through my teenage years, in the navy, and well into the practice of my profession. I quit high school in the ninth grade and was later forced by a judge to either enlist in the armed forces or go to reform school. When the navy forced me to take a GED test, I randomly checked answers without even reading the questions. Miraculously, I passed! In ministry, my arrogant air, unconsciously designed to cover my feelings of inadequacy, turned people off. They saw me as a supercontrolling, superconfident person on a big-time ego trip, and they were correct in their perceptions of my behaviors but not of my thoughts and feelings of self. I resisted everything and everybody just for the purpose of being obstinate, and in the process, I missed out on a lot of accept-ance I could have received.

I became a genuine *workaholic*. I went to school full time, ran a business of my own, preached every weekend, and then added flying lessons to that overload. I was known all over town as a very hard worker and actually received my first call to ministry because of it. It was all about proving my value and receiving "at-a-boys" from my mother whenever I did well financially on a carpet job. I needed to prove to myself that what was said to me as a child was a lie—I *could* amount to something! Bill, my brother-in-law, had demeaned and tormented me saying, "No Rockey will ever go to college. None of you have the brains to accomplish anything worthwhile." It was not until I had finished a Ph.D. that I realized my academic motives; the acquiring of degrees was to prove Bill wrong. What a price in stress I had paid to prove a point!

In ministry, I worked myself and Nancy nearly to death, attempting to prove myself to parishioners, conference officials, and all those who had said that I could never be anything but a loser. I dreamed up innovative plans for evangelism, for assisting couples in marital crisis, for having exciting and unusual worship services, and for being the most noticed pastor in the division.

I learned well how to *deny emotions*. I had the ability to reach somewhere inside myself where I would shut off my emotions like a water faucet. Even though I knew that I loved Nancy, when in an argument we would come to a certain point (probably when I began to feel defeated), all of a sudden I would turn on ice-cold emotions. Somehow I must have known that my coldness would undo her. And even though my great fear was of losing her, I could not acknowledge or communicate the truth. I would yell at her, "Don't let the door hit you on the backside on the way out. And just remember, if you leave, the door will be locked and you will never get back in."

When I felt a significant loss, I would ignore or deny my feelings, actually believing the lie I had told myself. But my emotions ignored, stuffed, or denied would come back around to haunt me with greater intensity at a later time. In my master's program, we were asked to make a time line of our intimacies and our losses, and I couldn't even recall one loss I had encountered in my life. It was Nancy who helped me recall one after another I had faced in my early childhood, ending with the death of my father—which I did not even chart on my assignment. The mind has a powerful mechanism for denying the truth that is too painful to remember yet which controls our thinking, feeling, and behaving. Nancy was usually the recipient of the rage I felt, blaming her for things she did not do. I had no idea of the true driving force behind my explosive rage.

The *indifference* I displayed toward Nancy must have been most painful to her. I tried to convince myself that I didn't care; that I would go on better without my sick, weak wife. I was good at preaching at her but would not share the tender feelings in my heart. I didn't know how; I had never been taught. When she was ill, I was disgusted and would be critical of her slow progress or would distance myself from her.

At one point I thought she was losing touch with reality, and I confess that I made a concerted effort to assist her by playing games with her mind. I knew she loved strawberry jam, so I hid it. Then when she was fumbling through the refrigerator and saying, "I thought we had some strawberry jam in here," I would play innocent, "Did we have strawberry jam? I don't remember any in the fridge!" I figured that if I helped her to go crazy, people would feel sorry for me, and I could then divorce her, marry someone better, and go on with my ministry. What sorrow those vivid memories cause me today!

People who are rejected in childhood often have a pre-conceived idea that everyone else in life will reject them, and tend to set up circumstances in such a way that they will get rejected, thus proving to themselves how rejectable they are. Others, in an unconscious attempt to not be rejected, will reject others first, and that's what I was doing with Nancy, with my children, friends, and colleagues.

Deep inside, my greatest fear was that Nancy would leave me for someone better. I feared her going on for graduate studies, because if she had a degree equal to mine and was better at our chosen profession, she wouldn't need me. I fooled myself into believing that my resistance to her getting a degree was because of the possibility that she might fail, and if she would I would have to endure the pain of her failure.

To protect myself I remained distant, unconnected, and uncommitted, and Nancy knew it. The pain she felt reminded her of the distance she felt from her dad during childhood, causing her to "know" that at some point in time, I would leave her. That fear created clinging behaviors on her part that turned me off and drove me further away. We were on a merry-go-round whose speed was increasing with every day's rejection felt, and we had no idea how to stop the spin.

We had thought that rejection was only one of the specific damages that occurs in childhood that arrests emotional development. Recently, however, we have come to believe that rejection goes beyond this. We believe that in addition to being a specific damage, it is also the result of all damages or abuses done to us. It is the result that Satan is actively working to create within each human being. He wants us to feel rejected and hopeless, just like he is. He purposes that we shall be rejected by family, friends, and ultimately, rejected by God. If he can accomplish that or help to create that assumption within us, he calculates one more subject added to his evil and hopeless kingdom.

Rejection is an insidious statement of personhood. It tells the recipient that they are not worthwhile, lovable, savable. Individuals who have no sense of hope for their future end up destroying self and others, thus accomplishing Satan's goal.

(Nancy) Ron and I almost did this. It came to the place in our experience where the lie that we were worthless had become so believable that we seriously considered ending our lives.

I recall sitting on the only "chair" in the only room of the house with a lock on the door. Somehow I was able to look at myself and analyze what was happening. There I was sitting in a fetal position, hugging myself and rocking myself back and forth for comfort. I recall saying to myself, "Look at you! Do you know what you are doing? As a nurse in the psychiatric unit you have seen people doing this many times. This is what crazy people do, so you must be one of them." Somehow I came to and realized that I had been in that room a long time, and I had better put on my plastic smile and continue my performance as if everything was OK.

Splashing cold water to hide my tears, I caught sight of myself in the mirror and Satan whispered in my ear, "You know what the problem is? God doesn't want you anymore. You must have done something so terrible that He has vowed to never use you again. You are rejected." My religious background had told me that to be rejected by God is death, so why live? In childhood I had looked to my father for acceptance and although it was there, he could not express it, and now my heavenly Father was silent.

(Ron) "I felt that Nancy was pulling away from me, and I didn't know why. First, it was my mother, and now another woman was abandoning me. The stressors of life—the business, the children, and now Nancy's despair—none of it made sense to me. But my reaction to this hopelessness didn't look like the typical depression I had learned about in my graduate studies.

The truth was that again I was in a position in life where I didn't belong; I didn't fit. I began to think, "The people in my life and the world around me don't understand who I am, so I might as well check out. It was like nobody understands and nobody cares, and I'm not worth anything anyway, and never have been, and everything I do I mess up, so my family, my wife, and my church would be better off without me."

Feelings of despair like these come in all shades. They come from sexual abuse, emotional abuse, physical abuse, and the abuse of rejection, which is the resulting core feeling from all damage and abuses done to us.

People who feel like misfits, whose relationships are unhealthy, who are dying for the want of touch and connection with another individual are all around us. Many have tried almost anything to feel relief, but it does not come. What we must understand is that change cannot take place without knowledge and understanding.

Our relief came as we expanded our understanding of Satan's deceptive plan to wound and warp children in their character-forming years, so that he can control them for life. The pathway to being released from the power of rejection is knowing the prison, discovering the escape route, and then taking the necessary steps toward the liberation of peace, love, and joy.

CHAPTER 7

Roots of Rejection

"Feelings buried alive never die."
Karol Kuhn Truman

His web is woven, the trap is in place; with each birth comes the opportunity for the spider to strike again. Satan's agenda is to trap every human being—and the earlier the better. And for too many it begins in the hospital nursery—if not before.

Two young parents press their noses against the glass of the nursery window scanning from one crib to another until they spot the one labeled with their name. Holding each other, they admire the little nose like Grandma's, the high forehead like Grandpa's, and the long fingers like Great grandma's. Thrilled with the life they have created, they excitedly plan the future. There will be Little League, piano lessons, and camping vacations in the mountains. They hope they can afford Harvard. Their intentions are pure, their ideals are lofty, and with everything in them they desire to be the most loving, supporting, influential parents, ever. They rehearse memories of their own childhood and vow that this child will never endure the pain that they felt.

If only they knew that behind the scenes the father of evil has for months been orchestrating the damage which they, as parents, or others will do to that little bundle of joy. Neither of them realize that the pain they experienced in childhood will be passed to their own child. Although they have read in their Bible about the sins of the parents being passed down, "unto the third and fourth generation . . ." (see Exod. 20:5), it is merely a cliché. They don't have major

SIN in their lives. They're "good" people who come from "good" families. Certainly this warning doesn't apply to them and the perfect little one their love has created. If they truly believed Scripture, before taking that little one from the hospital nursery, they would enroll in a Christian recovery program and earnestly begin working on their own issues. We all have them!

Current studies reveal that emotional pain, which parents themselves experienced prenatally and in their childhoods, gets passed on to their offspring in the DNA of body cells. Whatever damaging wounds the parents have received as children, their children also receive. It sounds hopeless, but it is not! Because even the most severely damaged human beings can experience recovery. What it takes is an individual who says, "Satan has damaged me and mine long enough. I will choose recovery. My garbage will not be passed on to the next generation. The cycle of abuse will stop with me."

The first step toward recovery is the knowledge of what circumstances may have happened to you that could have caused feelings of rejection. These same circumstances can cause your own children to feel rejected, so you must prevent, if possible, their occurrence. Here are the most common circumstances that can cause a child to feel rejected and what you can do to cushion the pain of rejection if the circumstance is unpreventable.

Divorce
A major portion of a child's security comes from a loving and healthy relationship between mother and father. When parents divorce each other, the children feel divorced. And children, especially young children, often conclude that the divorce was their fault. When divorce occurs, one parent or

the other usually gets custody of the children. The result is that children assume that the other parent has abandoned them. Childish thinking says, "If I can't see it, it doesn't exist." They ask over and over, "Where is Daddy?" or "Where is Mommy?" "Why did they leave me? What did I do that was so bad that they left?"

In order for children to be complete, the God-given software in the brain dictates that they need both male and female parents. For the first twelve years of the daughter's life she will model after Mommy. She will want to walk in Mommy's high heels, play with Mommy's pots and pans, and wear perfume and makeup just like Mommy.

During this time she does not realize that she is also learning from Daddy—just in a more subtle way. She is watching his responses to Mommy and his acts of kindness toward her. She needs the affirmation and compliments of the male figure in her life, so she begins to act in ways that she learns will bring this response from Daddy. At the onset of puberty, however, the focus of the daughter will shift toward her father, and from him she will receive validation, acceptance, guidance, and mentoring. Even her sense of spirituality comes through Daddy and his spiritual life.

The reverse is true for a male child. The focus will be on Daddy and modeling after him until the years of puberty, and then the focus will turn to Mommy, and he will learn how to treat a woman by interacting with her.

What happens when either of the parents is missing? The child misses out on that part of learning and maturing that should come as a result of observing and interacting with that person.

Dr. Laura Schlessinger, the internationally syndicated radio host who reaches 15 million listeners a week, takes a strong stand against divorce. Numerous times on her program she has stated emphatically that couples with children ought not to even consider the possibilities of divorce. Instead, they should get the help necessary to solve their personal and marital issues and commit for as long as they have children that they will be there as parents for their children.

If they have already divorced, then they ought to at least live near each other in the same town so both parents can have equal time with their children. Although it is important that children have a primary home and sleep in the same bed each night, it doesn't mean that the father can't pick the children up after school and fix supper for them. Children need both parents to be equally involved in their lives.

Sociologist Sarah McLanahan set out in the early nineties to prove that children raised by single parents were just as well off as those raised by two parents. What she found, however, shocked her. She realized she was wrong! "Children raised by single parents were twice as likely to be high school dropouts, give birth to out-of-wedlock children while still children themselves, develop drinking problems, and have a higher rate of divorce when they marry" (Dr. Laura Schlessinger, *How Could You Do That?!* [Harper Collins, 1996], 242).

Remarriage
Children often feel abandoned when divorce occurs, but their sense of rejection can be intensified with remarriage. Children often feel as if the remaining parent has formed a coalition with a stranger against their wish that the original parents will reunite.

Children want their "own" parents back. The method they use to accomplish their goal is to divide and conquer. They try every trick possible to make their stepparents miserable, hoping that they will leave, thus making it possible for the birth parents to return.

Complicating the home scene are new siblings who are also feeling out of place and desperately in need of love by parents who are trying to adjust to their new marriage. All of this creates fertile ground for major conflict and feelings of rejection.

Adequate time for being acquainted with each other prior to the marriage will help the children to establish a friendship. There should be time for picnics and trips to the zoo, working together around the house that will become their home, and conversation in which each child has input.

There should be quiet talks between each parent and their own children where the children are allowed to express their feelings regarding this new family.

Don't force the children to give up their bedrooms to the newcomers or share their belongings. Let the children help make the decision about who sleeps where and how each person can best have his or her needs met.

One of the most important topics of parental discussion should be regarding the discipline of the children. Does the new father have a right to discipline his new children? Does a stepmom have a right to discipline his kids? In every family a united parental front is important, but in stepfamilies, it is essential. If the children see a crack in the parental armor, they will take advantage of this, pushing in a wedge of contention that can easily drive the new couple apart—

and another marriage is destroyed. Make sure as parents you are secure enough in who you are and in your marriage relationship so that no child feels left out and that no child can drive you apart.

Parental fighting

Young children are intricately involved in everything they see, hear, or feel. If there is fighting going on around them, they assume that they are part of the fight or that they have in some way caused it. It's like children who watch a horror movie on TV and are scared the monster is going to stalk them rather than the little boy in the picture. Children respond emotionally as if it were happening to them.

Parents must learn to communicate with each other without evoking strong negative emotions or actions that can be frightening to children. There is no excuse for screaming, threatening, yelling obscenities, uttering demeaning accusations, throwing things, or looking disgusted. There is no excuse for pushing, pulling, slapping, or hitting. This is not the way mature individuals handle conflict. When children see their parents acting this way toward each other, it's just as if the abuse were happening to the child. In addition, the child will assume responsibility to either fix what is happening or protect the parent who receives the verbal or physical blows. Children in this situation become hyper-responsible, assuming responsibility for everything that happens around them. And because it is impossible for children to solve adult problems, the results are feelings of guilt and shame—the precursor to anxieties in later years.

"Fighting" in itself, if void of uncontrolled emotion and personal attack, is not all bad. Conflict is a part of all healthy relationships. But when parents do have disagreements in front of their children, it is very important that the children also see how the conflicts are resolved and how they can result in more understanding and a deeper commitment to each other.

Inconsistent discipline

Discipline based on parental mood or whim creates insecurity and multiple anxieties within children. Their security is to a large extent based on routine and that which is predictable. When children feel their parents can't be counted on to be consistent in their responses, their safety is threatened.

The first emotional task of children is the development of trust. But this is only possible in an atmosphere of predictability. If what seems OK today creates major crisis tomorrow, they are confused and anxious. They learn to read the attitudes and facial expressions of their parents and to sense the tension in the air when a parent is about to explode. They become fearful and distrustful; afraid that somehow what they say or do will cause parental wrath. Children then become imprisoned by their fear of the outcome of any choices they make and find it difficult to make decisions.

Inconsistent discipline gives children the message that they can never get it right. Discouragement results, and rather than try, many children retreat to the safety and privacy of their own world. Others put on an act. They feel they have to earn acceptance by their conformity, otherwise they are of little or no value. What is unfortunate here is that even their conformity does not earn them the acceptance they so desperately need. The main thing they learn is that they can never count on Mom or Dad.

Unmarried mother

Unmarried mothers come in several categories. There are those whose pregnancy was undesired—an accident due to unwise sexual contact. There are those who are so desperately seeking love that they submit sexually in order to hear the words "I love you," never thinking about the possible consequence of pregnancy. And there are those, especially girls in their teen years, who are so desperate to be needed and loved that they choose to have a baby, saying, "At last I have someone who needs me and loves me."

Little do teens realize the intense responsibility that children require. Who will do the feedings, who will sit up with the children when they are croupy, who will rock them, take them to Grandma's, and change a dozen dirty diapers a day?

One insightful seventeen-year-old who found herself pregnant and was devastated by the news made her decision to give the child for adoption. Her words were, "I can give birth to a child, but I cannot be a mother. I am too young; too much of life shining is ahead of me, and I haven't a clue as to how to be a good mother." She was mature enough to know that a mother was not just someone who gave birth. Rather, a mother has a responsibility twenty-four hours a day, seven days a week, for a lifetime.

What goes on in the mind of a teen who discovers she is pregnant? "How do I tell my parents? Can I just get an abortion with no one ever knowing and forget it like a bad dream? What about the father? Will he be supportive and loving and stay with me, or will he dump me like a used and outgrown toy? If I keep the baby, will my family babysit while I finish high school? Suppose they kick me out; where would I go? Where would I get the money for an abortion, or for a delivery?" Their internal turmoil is all-consuming. Finally she must face the music, tell her family and process through *their* pain and disappointment—as well as her own.

The mother in this situation feels disconnected from her family and friends, rejected by her lover; disowned and un-loved. And what the mother feels, the baby in utero will also feel. Her fears and anxieties are transferred to the un-born child. Many of these girls are driven to such despera-tion that suicide seems the best option. What happens to the baby when a mother attempts suicide? The baby in utero is affected by the medication she takes or the gas she in-hales, or just the rush of adrenaline, which is the result of her fear and anxiety.

After birth these feelings of rejection are intensified. She might be fascinated by the sight of what her body has pro-duced, but how can a lonely, unsupported child-mother be a place of calm and safety to her baby?

The trauma associated with an unmarried mother can be reduced when family and friends encircle her with love and acceptance. This pregnancy is not ideal; the circum-stances of conception was not God's plan, but each child, regardless of conception and birth, is a treasure to God and another opportunity for His grace and mercy to be revealed.

Damage can be reduced when the unmarried mother re-alizes that love is the God-given power of choice to do that which is in the best interest of another, regardless of her feel-ings. Mature decisions must be made on the baby's behalf.

An unwanted child
Many couples find it inconvenient to be pregnant when the dip stick turns pink or they get the plus sign. Emotions zoom out of control as couples face the reality of what has

happened to them; when they see their life plans shattered. The fallout hits the baby. While still in the womb, at about five and a half months gestation, infants begin to respond to their mother's emotions. The child who comes at a time when life's circumstances are confused will absorb from the mother her anxieties and fears and her apprehension at bringing a child into the world under these conditions.

At birth, during the critical bonding time, a mother in these circumstances can't display the same acceptance and adoration of the child had the circumstances been different. It may seem incomprehensible that a newborn can pick up these emotions, yet through their emotions is the one way they learn about their surroundings in the first days of life.

Babies perceive feeling before they have vocabulary or thought. Unwanted babies perceive that they are an inconvenience, that they are in the way, that it would have been better if they were never born. Some actually hear the words spoken from their parents' lips, "I wish you had never been born."

Some simply hear the parents telling the story of how difficult it was to bring a child into the world at their stage of life and are wounded anew each time the story of their birth is told.

Parents caught in this situation have only a few months in early pregnancy to put their lives in order and begin counting the blessings that this child is going to bring to them, before their rejection can damage their child.

A difficult birth

It has been discovered that children whose delivery was life threatening, where forceps were used, or where the baby became stuck in the birth canal will often have to deal with issues of rage. Where does the rage come from? From the perception that somebody is trying to kill me.

Recently in a seminar we were teaching, a female professional spoke to us during the break. "Finally I understand why my twin and I are so different. She was always such a mellow and agreeable child and I such a feisty and angry one. The truth is, no one expected twins. Moments after the birth of my sister, I was delivered breech. The cervix clamped down around my neck, leaving my head stuck in the uterus. Seconds before the life was chocked out of me, they were able to cut my mother enough to get me out. All my life I have felt a seething rage, totally unexplainable until now."

Good prenatal care is the best insurance against difficult births, but not all are preventable. Therefore, it's important to talk to your children about their births and explain how the origins of rejection could stem from birth trauma. Then reassure them of your love and acceptance.

Not bonding with parents at birth

Frequently circumstances, such as the critical illness of the baby or the mother, will occur that will cause the baby to be taken immediately from delivery to the nursery. The first two to four hours of life is the time the initial bonding takes place between parents and child. Babies look into their parents' faces and hope to see adoration mirrored back to them. If this does not occur, then the children may feel detached from the family and will blame themselves for that.

Illness of the child is not the only complication that can prevent bonding. Sometimes the mother goes through a delivery requiring anesthesia, and she remains drugged and asleep for a number of hours after birth. Years ago a medication called Scopolamine was given to women during the late stages of their labor, and with the injection came the information that the mother would not remember the birthing experience. This drug, in combination with pain medication, was capable of sedating a woman for six to ten hours while the baby slept alone, tightly snuggled in the nursery blanket. The mother's own state of health, both psychological and physical, can be a contributing factor to her ability to bond with her newborn.

The ideal would be for every mother to be able to deliver without general anesthesia or drugs that would produce sedation and for the baby to be given to mother to touch and adore immediately after birth.

During those critical two to four hours after birth, the primary concern is that the baby bonds with mother and ideally with the father. This helps to establish with the child his or her sense of identity and his connection to a mother and a father. In addition, it is good to have older siblings and grandparents there. When this happens the baby can begin to put faces with the voices heard while in the womb. It is during this bonding time that the baby begins to perceive that these significant people are his/her family. "I belong here, and I am wanted."

Adoption

Adopted children may lack the words to express their feelings of emptiness and unconnectedness they feel being separated from a birth mother, even though their adoptive family has nurtured and adored them. Some adoptive parents fear the moment when the child they love will announce a desire to find the "real" parents. The child seeks answers to these questions: "Why did my mother give me away? What were the circumstances of her life that forced her to that choice? What was so bad about me that I was rejected?"

Once the answers are found, most children will be satisfied and will move on with their lives, allowing their feelings of rejection to diminish. Some may choose to build a relationship with birth parent(s), but if they do, the majority will retain a special bond of love with the family they've been a part of all their lives.

The way to assist adopted children in feeling less rejected is to cooperate with them in their desire to find the original parents and not to be threatened by their need to connect with their beginnings.

If a young woman is struggling with the decision of whether or not to keep her child or give her child to adoptive parents, she should know that if she chooses adoption, there is a process she can implement that will reduce the possibility of her child having a permanent emptiness where the birth mother should be.

Maggie was only sixteen when she became pregnant, and because she didn't feel she was capable of providing the home she wanted for her baby, she decided to give her baby for adoption. Through the contact of friends, an adoptive family was located across the continent, and arrangements were made. Letters and phone calls allowed a friendship to grow between Maggie and the adoptive parents, Bill and Darcy. When the time for delivery came, Bill and Darcy flew into town and were met at the airport by the birth grandparents. A few days later the adoptive grandparents flew into town, and the two families bonded with each other over the supper table for a number of days while they awaited the arrival of this special child.

In the delivery room Maggie's mom and a close family friend, who was a nurse, coached Maggie through the very difficult birthing process, while Bill and Darcy sat immediately outside the delivery room door anticipating the first cry. Maggie had been prepared that in order to fill a void within the mind of her newborn, she would need to bond with her in those first moments after birth. So Maggie held little Linda close, whispered words of endearment and love, and explained the reason why she had chosen to give her to a whole and healthy mother and father. After about six or seven minutes of gazing into her baby's eyes and caressing her, and with her legs still in stirrups, she asked for the adoptive mother to come into the delivery room. When Darcy came in, Maggie said, "Come, here is your baby. A beautiful little girl." The two mothers reached out and held each other with that precious baby between them, and tears flowed.

As soon as the doctor had finished her repair, the new daddy was summoned into the room. For the next thirty-six hours the three parents cared for the little one together; rocking, feeding, and loving her.

Upon the baby's release, the two families went to the church where they were met by supportive family and friends and they participated in a baby dedication ceremony and the official transferring of parental rights to Bill and Darcy. A scrapbook was prepared with pictures of Maggie as a child and the birth family, along with letters Maggie had written to her baby while she was pregnant. When Linda is ready, the scrapbook will confirm the love that it took to make the choice to give her away. Each week Maggie talks to her child over the phone and sends letters and pictures.

Some people limit a baby's capacity to love, thinking the baby must either love the birth parents or the adoptive parents. But God has given each child the capacity to love both. It's up to the birth parents and the adoptive ones to cooperate in creating an environment where this love can be nurtured.

Parents who are abusive to their children or each other

If acceptance is so important that babies are looking for it during the early hours of their lives, then it becomes even more important during the early childhood years. In order for children to grow up psychologically healthy, they must have acceptance. How would these children interpret physical pain, humiliation, sexual abuse, and verbal putdowns? Certainly not as acceptance! Instead, they perceive that they must be very bad for these things to happen to them.

It is easy to see why children who have been abused feel rejected. Yet, many parents have no idea that the way they are treating their children is causing psychological pain. That's why parenting classes are so important.

It's also a fact that abuse to another sibling or to a parent can cause a child to feel rejected. Children cannot separate themselves from other family members. When injustice happens to one, it's as if it happened to them as well. Children watching abuse feel the emotional blows when the parent or siblings are receiving the physical ones.

When a parent is abused, children often assume that they are the cause of the abuse to the other parent. In other words, "If Daddy is beating Mommy, it must be because of me."

Vicki was one of those children. When she was just a toddler she recalls standing beside her little bed, her body stiff as a board and shaking from head to toe as she listened to the sounds of her mother being bounced off the walls in the next room. After episodes like this, she knew that Mother would hide herself in her room for a couple days, and there would be no one but the older sisters to take care of her. On several occasions the older sisters, tiring of the responsibility of caring for their little sister, would lock Vicki in the outside shed until Mom came out of hiding. Her food would come from a little neighborhood girl who would sneak candy through the cracks in the shed. Talk about rejected! This little girl was being punished by what Daddy was doing to Mommy. You can see how easy it would be for her to interpret that she was the cause of Mother's beatings.

If you feel that abuse is taking place in your home, or in any other home, you have a moral and legal responsibility to report what you know or suspect is happening at that home. Call Child Protective Services in your area, and they will handle your report confidentially. If nothing gets done by the authorities, then somehow get to the child who is being abused and build a friendship. It is important that the child has a safe person to talk to and a safe place to go if the abuse should continue. You may be the only place of safety and the only confidant that child has. Continue to report the abuse over and over again until some legal action is taken to protect the child.

If the abuse is happening to an adult, go to that person and say, "I sense that you are being mistreated. I just want you to know that I am here to be supportive of you. And I also want you to know that you are valuable and should not be treated in this way. What help can I give to you so that you have the courage to remove yourself from the abuse and get the help both of you need so this does not need to continue?"

Parental drug and alcohol addiction

Addictions are all-consuming. They become primary in the life of an addictive parent, and a child learns quickly that if it comes to a choice between the bottle or the baby, the chances are good that the addict will choose the bottle. Numbed out on drugs, the parent may be physically present but emotionally absent.

If you use the definition of love as "My God-given power of choice to do that which is in the best interest of another, regardless of my feelings," then it is obvious that a parent who is an addict loves his or her addictions more than the child.

The bonding that should take place between the parent and child is sabotaged because the parent's true self is hidden under the mask of medication. Someone who is high on marijuana or angry from alcohol or asleep from drugs is unavailable to the child. The entire family finds itself dancing around the condition or the mood of the addicted. While the parent should be the responsible one, roles are reversed and the child takes responsibility for the parent. Childhood is ripped away when the child is prematurely forced into adult responsibilities. The parental message the child receives is "I don't want you to be who you are—just a child. I want you to be responsible for me. I reject the child; I want the adult."

The only way out of this situation is for the parents to face the issues that drive them to escape reality and to get the help they need to break their addictions.

Some children have never enjoyed the innocence and freedom of childhood joy because of regular harsh treatment or being ignored by parents. Scolding, beating, and constant put-downs have destroyed the ability to trust and speak honestly. Instead, fear, envy, jealousy, and decietfulness have been adopted as defensive behaviors.

Older parents who look back over their parenting years may ask themselves, "Why is my teen or adult child hurting so much?" The chances are great the child is suffering from one or more of the circumstances that typically cause feelings of rejection, such as divorce, remarriage, parental fighting, inconsistent discipline, an unmarried mother, an unwanted child, a difficult birth, the inability to bond at birth, family violence, adoption, or parental drug and alcohol addiction.

But even if a specific circumstance can't be pinpointed as the causal agent, this does not discount the rejection. If an older child or adult feels rejected, *they were rejected*. No amount of arguing about it or trying to prove what good parents you were will change this perception. Only when the child feels your total acceptance, even though his or her behavior may be hurtful to you, will these feelings of rejection be defused. Regardless of age, the person feeling rejection needs to be given permission to talk about their feelings without having them discounted or told how foolish it is to feel that way. Your understanding and sympathy is the best prescription for their recovery.

CHAPTER 8

The Seeds That Produce Resentment Weeds

"Those who are called to suffer for Christ's sake,
who have to endure misapprehension and distrust,
even in their own home, may find comfort in the thought
that Jesus has endured the same."
Ellen G. White

Injustices are the seeds of resentments that develop throughout life and color the success of relationships, careers, and even one's spirituality. Resentment is defined as a feeling of indignant displeasure or persistent ill will at something regarded as a wrong, insult, or injury.

Were your needs ignored and your desires sabotaged by another's agenda? Were your words and acts of kindness received with a "you owe me" attitude instead of a Thank you? Maybe you find that your best intentions are often misinterpreted. Perhaps you're the one who "always" picks up the dirty laundry and pays the bills and then gets blamed when something isn't "right!" Or maybe people are always *telling* you what to do instead of *asking*. Resentment is what you feel each time you perceive you've been used and taken advantage of! Because of the anger seething inside, you find yourself complaining "through your teeth" with clenched jaw and angry tone.

Fear of reprisal often acts to keep the resentment lid on, like a damper is used to lower the inside flame of a woodburning stove. However, the seldom understood truth is that dampers also increase the heat on the inside! Accompanying each use of the "damper" is an increase in the intensity of your anger. The day comes when you can no longer tolerate the heat. It is then that you explode in rage and burn everyone around you with your searing words.

If you honestly examine the thoughts and feelings that surround your reservoir of resentments, you will probably find, at the core of your feeling, a sense of having been rejected, slighted, ignored, or discounted. Somehow you got the feeling that everyone else was more important than you. You didn't matter. You have no worth and value.

Resentments do not build overnight, just as a reservoir does not fill instantly or a seed grow to maturity in a day. Slowly over a period of time, the mind adds up the injustices done to it, labels them "rejection," and begins to feel the anger that rejection produces. But once the reservoir is filled—once the seeds are mature—BEWARE. The monologue shouting in the mind, fueled by just one more injustice, can erupt in an outburst, creating such a mighty fire that it rages out of control. Most people fearing such a catastrophic event bury their feelings deep within. And the result? A deeper reservoir, more resentment seeds, and a hotter fire that destroys from the inside out.

We are all vulnerable because of injustices done to us. To avoid this scenario, many find it a full-time job to manage their emotions. They reason that if they can just keep themselves busy enough, they won't have to think about their pain, their anger, their fear, or their sadness. So they work, they exercise, they perform, they do good, and they hop from one project to the next, avoiding and ignoring.

Daniel Goleman, in his book *Emotional Intelligence*, suggests that emotionally sound infants learn to soothe themselves by treating themselves as their caretakers have treated them, leaving themselves less vulnerable to the upheavals of the emotional brain. Since in adulthood we continue the patterns learned in early childhood, we practice such self-destructive behaviors as not crying or crying all the time in an attempt to keep our minds from thinking or our mouths from speaking of the situation. We might even choose to "veg," doing nothing at all, hoping that our feelings, if ignored, will go away. Some go to the extent of denying that they even have feelings, or if they do, find themselves incapable of identifying them.

When our emotions have filled our reservoir because we have frozen, ignored, and denied their existence, then the destructive process begins internally. This process can be directed outward, destroying others with our condemnatory judgments, biting comments, criticisms or cynicism, or they can produce malignant results on the inside, including physical ailments, anxieties, obsessions, compulsions, or depression.

If this process sounds like something you've been battling, then it's important to take a closer look at the beginnings of resentments. Here are ten "seeds" that produce resentment "weeds."

1. Growing up in an atmosphere of criticism

Many children are raised in homes where a critical spirit or attitude prevails. Maybe in your family everyone was criticized. The mail carrier *never* came at the right time, the neighbors had "no taste" because they planted fewer flowers than your family, your aunties were "too fat," your grandparents "too nosey," the pastor "too long-winded," and his wife "too bossy."

Were all the members of your household judged—and found lacking? Because children do not easily identify a boundary between themselves and others, the criticism that is heaped on others is internalized by children as if it belonged to them.

Perhaps as a child, you grew up thinking that nothing you did was ever done right. Maybe you heard something like this, "You did it OK, but . . ." No matter how well you cleaned the house, mowed the lawn, cared for your room, or did your homework, the authorities in your family—the people who mattered most to you—seldom gave you credit or acknowledged your accomplishments.

Is your tendency today to have an opinion about every aspect of everyone's life? Do you find yourself making judgment calls on the behaviors of others, which you may or may not communicate to them? Can you always find the flaw—the tiny thing that's wrong in some project you or someone else has done? Do you find yourself consistently rejecting your work or another's? If you answer Yes to any of these questions, your behavior is normal for having been raised in a criticizing atmosphere, but it doesn't have to stay that way! You don't have to plant weeds of rejection in the lives of others!

There's truth in this jingle by Mildred Howells, reprinted in The Illustrated Bible, 1275:

> *"And so it criticized each flower,*
> *This supercilious seed;*
> *Until it woke one summer hour,*
> *And found itself a weed."*

Growing up with criticism has other negative spinoffs. Your tendency is probably to feel unsatisfied with your accomplishments. Since whatever you did wasn't good enough, you may now feel you aren't entitled to even take a risk or try something new, for if you did risk and fail, or you did try something new and it was unsuccessful or unacceptable, you would be rejected too—just like "aunty," the neighbors, or the preacher and his wife.

So, in an effort to combat the feelings of worthlessness, you . . .

- *Work too much*, because you feel that if you could just do enough, you might feel satisfied or accomplished, and others might eventually sit up and notice.

- *Are a perfectionist,* because you must try to avoid criticism at any cost; it hurts too much! You want to be thought of as capable and worthwhile, so you drive yourself. And too often you drive others to achieve your same perfectionistic goals, erroneously believing that their accomplishments, or lack of them, will somehow reflect on you.

- *Procrastinate*, because it's safer to put off things until you know you'll be successful. Sometimes even thinking about a project paralyzes you with the fear of failure.

- *Sabotage your own success*, because the risk of failure screams louder than the promise of success.

- *Never feel successful*, but you keep working at it, because working itself is noble and is seldom criticized. If nothing else, you'll at least be considered industrious.

- *Settle for second best.* You tell yourself, "That's good enough for me!" When your personal value is low, you settle for less in life.

Parents do not realize the profound effect that the criticism of those in authority, such as parents or religious leaders, has upon children. When children live with criticism, they learn to criticize rather than respect authority figures in the family, school, and society. As children grow, this attitude of criticism can extend to God, who is our ultimate authority, thus making unbelievers of them.

2. Comparison with siblings, friends, and others

How often did you hear that you should be more like your brother or sister? Maybe your family compared you to family members, friends, or other kids in your school? Perhaps you heard "When I was a kid, we were very poor and I had to . . ." In that context, your advantage or privilege was being contrasted to that of a parent or older person. You were subtly being demeaned because of when and under what circumstances you were born. Some children caught in this flood of criticism end up feeling that they are somehow responsible for other people's disadvantages.

If comparisons with others was a habit in your family, your worth and value as a unique, special individual was lessened with each comparison.

In chapter 6, I (Nancy) tell about being about eight or nine years old and failing miserably at a piano recital. I was absolutely paralyzed by fear because my dad, an accomplished pianist himself, sat anxiously expecting a perfect performance. I had heard my father sigh in disgust when I returned to my seat humiliated. Then the planned stop for ice cream on the way home was bypassed, and we drove in silence. I curled in the corner of the back seat, fearfully anticipating the worst. About one mile from home, Dad finally came out with it. "I wish I knew what was wrong with you. Why in the world can't you play like _____)?" (He named a childhood chum.)

I made no response. What was there to say. I had no idea why I couldn't play or that fear had blocked my ability to think; to remember. I recall just slinking farther down into the seat, feeling utterly worthless and hopeless. I wanted to play the piano, I really did, but fear blocked creativity and sabotaged my ability.

My childhood chum is still my friend. We grew up together in the same duplex and attended the same elementary and high school and even went to the same college. I have, however, always felt inferior to her, and in college we drifted apart. We are always happy to see each other, but I have wondered if my dad's unfair comparison of us is why I haven't chosen to stay closer through the years. What a loss!

The tendency of those who are compared with others is to perform in some different noncompetitive area in order to get the affirmation needed. Some lean toward materialism—a need to acquire possessions designed to make them look good. Comparing themselves with others in appearance, abilities, or possessions will drive them to achieve far beyond what is sensible or necessary, just to prove their value. All this leads to a competitive spirit, which may or may not manifest itself on the surface.

The internal drive to excel, to accomplish, to surpass others creates a burden of stress that inevitably drains energy, so that intimate relationships end up paying the price. The energy used to hide the truth, to maintain a guard, or keep a reserve saps the vital life forces and takes its toll on the physical body as well as on the mind.

Take a few minutes to recall if you were compared to others during your childhood. Who were they? Who was doing the comparing? What feelings do you have toward those to whom you were compared? Look at your tendencies today. Do you tend to be materialistic, overly competitive, or feel less valuable than others? If so, perhaps you need to hand back the lie that was intimated regarding your worth and value in the process of those comparisons. That lie had the power to control your thoughts, feelings, and behaviors, and it's real origin was with the father of lies. Give it back to him! Then remember this principle: "Let everyone be sure that he is doing his very best, for then he will have the personal satisfaction of work well done, and won't need to compare himself with someone else" (Gal. 6:4, TLB).

3. Absence of emotional connection with parents

Unlike a family where parents are missing or absent, families suffering from the absence of emotional connections have the physical presence of both parents. But psychologically absent parents, those who are around but refuse to interact, can sometimes arouse more childhood resentment than those who are physically absent.

Perhaps your dad was a workaholic, and you seldom saw him unless he was going to or returning from work. Or when he was home, was he so tired that he was zoned out? It might be that he spent the majority of his time either behind the newspaper or a book, in front of the television, or doing work for the church. Was your mother the superwoman mom who baked all her own bread; canned fruit and vegetables; made jams, jellies, and pickles; and seemed to spend all her waking moments in the kitchen? You might have loved the results of her labors, but did you ever wish that you could have sacrificed some of them for a few moments of her undivided attention? Were you one of the many who were damaged outside the home and chose to not tell your parents of the event(s), because you feared they'd blame you? Did you feel that you were in the way or just an irritant in the house—a fly in the ointment?

In a home where parents are unavailable emotionally or refuse to listen to their children, the children are deprived of the intimate connection that is a requirement for the full development of a healthy mind. There is a principle that should be understood here: When we find ourselves frequently making others wrong and maintaining our rightness, we sacrifice the privilege of intimacy. Children need to be not only heard but also to be emotionally understood. Parents who will take the time to listen actively, reading between the lines and questioning until the child's feelings are understood and accepted, reap the benefit of emotional intimacy with their children. This prepares the children to feel comfortable in sharing anything that's going on in their lives, positive or negative. The child finds a safe place in the heart of the parent and will willingly and confidently share life's secrets at this place of safety and security.

The absence of emotional connection in early childhood prepares the heart for a lack of trust and the fear of commitment in friendships and in marriage. The child begins to feel devalued and unworthy of an equitable relationship with another person. It may be that another adult may have connected with the child and there the child found a place of acceptance. However, the lack of parental connection leaves children with a hole in their hearts.

How can we expect to be intimate with a God we cannot see, hear, or touch if parents who were physically present could not connect? Our experience with our parents and our attitude toward them is reflected in our relationship with God.

In marriage, the inability to connect emotionally becomes threatening to the life of the relationship. Women, whose primary need is for emotional fulfillment, will starve in a marriage with a husband who is out of touch with feelings. In today's society, men frequently express their need and desire for emotional intimacy with their wives, but if the woman's strength and energy is drained by the demands of career and home, the soft and tender woman becomes a machine.

The world abounds with examples of this pain and has been proclaimed to the public in the exposure of the private lives and lack of intimacy between Charles, the Prince of Wales, and his late wife, Princess Diana. The childhood of the princess was one of absolute loneliness and lack of connection with parents. Then the formality of the royal family overshadowed the intimacy Diana so greatly desired to have with her children and her husband. In their marriage, each suffered from the need for intimacy and the inability to connect with each other.

The person whose feelings are frozen has denied himself/herself the right to feel or to question. Mistrust for others is developed early in childhood, producing in its wake the fear of vulnerability. Many actually choose to live in a controlling atmosphere, having become used to someone else having all the feelings and making all the decisions.

With whom did you connect as a child on an emotional level? Who was the safest and most accepting person in your life? With whom did you share the joy and the pain of your life? With whom do you share now? You don't have to have dozens of friends, but emotional health demands at least one healthy emotional connection!

The internal struggles with feelings of rejection can surface in every circumstance and experience of life. We expect that people will reject us, and when they don't, we will behave in such a manner that they will. We will push people to extremes seeing exactly what it will take for them to reject us. "If I do this, will you still love me; will you still accept me?"

While on the inside we have a desperate longing to be intimately connected with at least one human being, on the outside our behaviors are designed to push people away. Fear predicts its own end, and the fear of being rejected often finds its fulfillment at some point in the life. Thus confirming that what we expected is what we get.

(Ron) I was the skinniest kid on the block, teased and tormented. As a teen, I was a loner who desperately needed to bond and could find no partner. I paid for my intimacies. That way I could just leave them and not feel the pain of rejection. The desperate need in my life was to have the father emptiness filled. All along the way God provided for me a substitute, but it was not until I made the choice to be willing to look at my damage and to process through it that I was able to feel relief from the pressure. That relief put me in touch with the Father. Regardless of my thoughts, feelings, or my behaviors, His love is constant. Once I accepted that, I began to accept the love of my wife and feel love for her. Loving my children was the next step. I continue to learn what freedom is.

4. Discounting of feelings

"It's a sin to be angry." "Only babies are afraid of . . . " "Big boys don't cry!" Did any of these emotional denials become the rules to live by that have made it unsafe for you to express your feelings?

Perhaps you were not allowed to feel proud of anything you'd accomplished. Maybe your family wouldn't allow you to feel sad, glad, or mad! It's not uncommon for us to be told that the depth of pain we feel is far greater than it should be. "Just stop your bellyaching; it's not that bad!" You may have been told that your pain was not important, and you were forced to put up with it without assistance or relief. What was important was that you acted "right" regardless of your feelings. In fact, there was little or no concern for what you were feeling!

Receiving this type of treatment while our characters are being formed diminishes our sense of value and importance. As we grow toward adulthood, the tendency to hide or deny our feelings increases, until many say that they have no feelings at all. Others seem to take their cue of how to feel from people around them and act accordingly. This behavior is designed to guarantee acceptance by peers, but the true self is denied, and thus relationships are superficial.

In adulthood, these grown-up children have learned to deny that they have feelings. As a result, they tend to lead mundane lives, void of passion and intimacy.

Who in childhood told you that your feelings were foolish? Are you currently able to feel your feelings, label them, and then share them with another? With whom do you share? Where is your safe emotional harbor?

5. Abusive touch

Louise, a very sensitive and caring schoolteacher, told of her recent experience on the first day of a new school year. She stood at the door of her classroom to greet the new children assigned to her room, and as each arrived, she introduced herself, asked their name, and affectionately placed her hand on the child's shoulder.

One unkempt boy introduced himself as Todd, and as Louise gently laid her hand on his shoulder, he jerked himself away shouting, "Ouch! You're hurting me!"

"Today," she said, "two weeks into the school year, as I read the morning story with the children sitting on the floor around me, Todd lay with his head in my lap. With one hand I held the book and with the other I stroked his head. I found out that his mother carried around a large, metal spoon with her, with which she would thunk his head whenever he said or did something annoying. He has found a safe place in my lap where every morning he lays his head to receive the gentle affection he's dying for."

Those who have endured abusive touch in childhood tend to either shrink from touch of any kind or will themselves become the playground bully; pushing, shoving, and hitting; copying the behavior they have seen at home. Sadly enough, those who came from childhoods where they have suffered abusive touch often choose a life partner who will continue this behavior. Some will become perpetrators of physical abuse to their partners or children. Others will withdraw from any physical contact because of fear. Sexual frigidity or abusiveness in sexual behaviors is not uncommon in these relationships.

Many tell the stories of severe physical punishments they received in childhood and even seem to be bragging that they survived the torture. These folk have learned to separate their feelings from the facts. Because of the emotional pain attached to the experiences, it is far greater than they can tolerate. This is known as *dissociating* and is a tool for survival frequently associated with sexual abuse at a young age. Many victims of incest or molestation will recall the incidents but share how they were able to remove themselves to another place from which they watched the abuse being perpetrated on the child. They will say that it is the only way they could tolerate the physical as well as the emotional agony. Sexual frigidity or its opposite, promiscuousness, is not uncommon in those who have been so damaged.

Did you suffer the torture of abusive touch? How do you tend to treat others with whom you are in relationship today? Do you shrink away from touch completely because you're afraid that you will hurt another? Or do you find yourself administering the same painful blows that you felt as a child?

6. The absence of touch

"The day I learned to walk on my own is the last day I was picked up," Mike told us sadly. "My family were like the bumper cars one can ride at a fair. The only touch we got was if we accidentally bumped into each other passing on the stairway."

I (Ron) replied. "My brother George was forever being touched, but the touch he got was from Dad's razor strap. I used to wonder why George got all the attention and I got none. Even though George's furnace room beatings were so severe that he would sob half the night, I often wondered why I was so bad that I couldn't get all that attention. Finally by the time I was in third grade, I discovered that if I was 'bad enough,' I could get that attention from my teachers."

(Nancy) "I remember how Ron reacted to touch on our honeymoon. Just coming off the ferry we had taken to our honeymoon island, he fell on the dock and sprained his ankle. Being a nurse and a nurturer, I ran to him and put my arms around him. He was sitting on the dock, squeezing the ankle when I approached, and his arms flew out as he hollered, "Get away from me! Leave me alone when I'm hurting!" What a shock! As a nurse who had helped many in pain, I had never had a patient react to me like that! I knew that his childhood had been lonely and without affection, and I figured that he'd gratefully drink in all the physical affection I could give him. Boy, was I wrong! Even in our intimate moments, he felt smothered by my attentions, since touch was foreign to him. The caressing felt abusive to him because he had not known it before. Sexuality begins in infancy when a baby is bathed, massaged with lotion, cuddled, or gently rocked. A person whose infant experiences did not include this physical tenderness will grow up to avoid it in adulthood.

In the intimacy of marriage, such a person will feel controlled or smothered by touch, even when desirous of sexual expression with their mate. Once the partner has become accustomed to touch, however, he or she may demand that all of the years robbed of childhood touch be compensated for by the spouse. If this happens, the marriage can easily slip into a codependent relationship where the affectionate partner becomes a surrogate parent. In this manner, the "child" finally receives the affirmation desired.

However, no husband or wife can really compensate for the deprivation of childhood. Many such adults, starving with skin hunger, expect their partner to fill their void, but the void will remain, and the spouse will be accused of a lack of affection and touch. They will fear rejection and abandonment by their partner, but at the same time they can't understand or provide commitment to their partner. Overpossessiveness is common in these relationships.

Adding to the confusion are behaviors that do not match the need. Such partners long to be touched, yet they keep their spouses at a distance by absenting themselves from the home (to work, to play, or for many other excuses), yet their mate MUST always be at home and physically and emotionally available at all times.

Who was your safe place for touch in childhood? Can you recall snuggling with someone for long periods of time,

gently being caressed and held? Was your safe person someone in your home, or did you have to find that safety in
someone outside of your immediate family?

7. Shaming your body

"No man is ever going to want you, you're too fat!" "You'll
be old unless you do something about your ugly teeth," "Hey,
little shrimp," "Fatso," "Four eyes," "Skinny Minnie." All
these are names or slurs meant to demean or embarrass
another because of some body flaw or unique difference. Did
you hear any of these as a kid? Perhaps you heard other
names, sing-song rhymes, or derogatory comments made
about you and your body.

I (Nancy) remember being told by a religious leader that
I would have to do something about my ugly teeth if I expected to marry a minister and go anywhere in our denomi-
nation. After the birth of our second daughter, Naomi, three
teeth "died" and I pleaded with my dentist to do a whole
upper denture instead of a bridge to replace three teeth.
Today I owe my smile to my dentist.

Attitudes displayed and words said regarding our bodies seem to play over and over in our minds like a record
stuck in a groove. This replay determines our actions for
years to come. It creates an internal struggle to look and
act perfect. We become obsessive about our appearance and
will go to great lengths to look acceptable. The tendency is
to compare ourselves to others and seek affirmation from
others. While we desperately need words of praise and ac-
ceptability, when we hear them, we can be so set in the "ugly"
rut that we refuse to believe they are true.

Many who have had their bodies shamed have an excessive fear of aging. They fear they won't look acceptable in
older years. Looking unacceptable is part of the pain of im-

pending rejection to those who are sensitive in this area due to earlier trauma.

It is important that you understand that the pendulum of behavior swings in both directions, just like the pendulum of a clock swings from left to right, and it doesn't matter which side it's on to tick the clock, so the behaviors can vary from one extreme to another and still stem from the same need. While some become overly concerned about their appearance, for others who feel rejected, their appearance is sadly neglected.

What will it take for you to accept yourself as God's creation and sing with the psalmist, "I will praise You, for I am fearfully and wonderfully made; Marvelous are Your works" (Psalm 139:14, NKJV)?

8.   Shame created by the behavior of parents

Were you a son who had to go to the bar on weekends to drag your father home? Or were you the daughter who was embarrassed by your mother's provocative behaviors with the teacher or the boys in your classroom? Maybe your parents never attended your school functions or always argued loudly at the grocery store. Or perhaps you were humiliated because, after having a succession of affairs that everybody seemed to know about, they divorced. Or were you devastated by the fact that your parents were the only parents who seldom, if ever, attended school or church functions in which you had a part?

Children who grow up under such circumstances have difficulty trusting authority figures or persons who feel like authorities to them. Often, even as adults, we will feel that we don't have the right to belong. We feel we don't have the right to have a healthy, happy family.

Often, because self-worth is diminished in such situations, materialism is substituted for inner value. The tendency is to feel that no one cares about you, and even when love comes your way through a spouse, children, or friends, you can't quite believe that their love is true. Even when family and friends are reliable, your tendency is to believe that you'll be hurt, disappointed, things won't work out, or you'll be abandoned. In short, you fear that you'll be rejected again, and all too often, your expectations are realized. Fears are often predictions of the future that unconsciously we arrange.

In many cases, children, whose parents' behavior is shameful, have to take on the responsibility of a parent toward their parent whose actions are childish. That heavy load places a burden upon the children that emotionally they are unable to bear and, in adulthood, anxieties are a sure result.

It is also true that adults whose family of origin was an embarrassment often feel they don't have the right to belong to a family, or resist belonging, so that history will not repeat itself. Often in adulthood, grandiose ideas will haunt the mind, just like they did in childhood, when the child fantasized that Mom or Dad would not humiliate them "this time." Feelings of being damaged and different from others, not being part of the "in crowd," and insecurities and chronic distrust of self and others is common. Because others cannot be trusted, there is often a need to control the environment, schedules, habits, and even decisions of others.

9. Expecting children to know without proper instruction or the time to learn

Picture the scene: You take out the old push lawn mower on a sweltering summer afternoon just to surprise your dad with a freshly cut lawn when he arrives home from work. You've never cut the lawn before, and you know he wouldn't allow you to ride the tractor mower like he does, so you do it the hard way. Just as you have made the last swipe across the front lawn, you hear his truck coming down the road, so you quickly run with the mower to the garage. The perspiration is pouring down your face as Dad comes in the drive, and you anticipate a look of surprised pleasure. But he says nothing. At the supper table he asks, "What's the deal, Son? Were you too lazy to mow the backyard?"

Maybe it happened that with insufficient practice, you were expected to perform for some social event and were humiliated by forgetting your lines or botching the musical notes. The pain of embarrassment that was too much to handle was further accentuated by your parents' verbal putdowns. Or were you expected to do a task perfectly the very first time you attempted it? Were you disappointed by your first attempt at baking a cake when it fell just moments after taking it out of the oven and then had to endure your family's unmerciful teasing and chiding because of your failed attempt?

The adult years, after such childhood experiences, are marked with fear—fear of trying new things that you'd never tried before, fear of expected punishment, fear of making a mistake with the resulting insults and laughter adding to the pain of your failure.

Internally you might suffer a haunting sense of inferiority, a "knowing" that you aren't and never will be good enough. Of course, the question might be asked, "Good enough for what?" And you would answer, "Good enough for Mom and Dad; good enough for everybody: good enough for God."

If you were hit with this seed of resentment, the tendency could be toward perfectionism, an attempt at getting it right at all costs. It may well be that you would pretend to be ignorant, act as though you can't perform the task or do the job, while you have the ability to do it as well or better than anyone else. Life might be plagued by anxieties, fears for the future, fears of having your "inept self" revealed, fears that whatever you accomplish will be done poorly or inadequately and you will never meet up to the expectations you have set for yourself.

10. Conditional acceptance

One of the most serious and deeply disturbing wounds of childhood is the feeling of being only conditionally accepted by the significant others in your life. The chances are great, however, that you were loved regardless of what you did, but the problem is that the messages you received got scrambled. You caught messages that said, "You're only loved when you get good grades, make your bed, brush your teeth, and say Please and Thank you." What scrambled these messages of unconditional acceptance? Their negative emotions—their criticism, anger, neglect, or looks or words of disappointment. When acceptance from parents felt conditional, its impact on you was the most powerful because those who should be nurturing to a child have the potential for the most invasive harm. And the result is that the little seeds of resentment begin to take root.

If you're thinking you weren't accepted by your parents for the person you were as a child but were only accepted when you were "good," it's time for another look. Perception is powerful because it becomes our reality. One or two instances of feeling rejected, especially by parents, has the power to color our view of all their feelings toward us. Children are supersensitive to attitudes, tone and pitch of voice, and facial expressions, thus easily misinterpreting disappointment as disapproval.

Please do not misunderstand. Some do accept others only on the basis of performance, and such behavior is certainly contrary to the character of an all-loving God. Parents who thus treat their children are giving them the powerful message that God accepts them only when they are "good boys and girls." Since the requirement of obedience without a relationship produces rebellion, it is easy to understand how children thus treated can rebel against an earthly parent or their heavenly Father.

The most important step you can take is to be willing to look within yourself to see how your early years have impacted your life then and continue doing so today. What was then, is now. Maintaining a teachable spirit or asking God to give you one will open you to understand how what you think and feel today was orchestrated by what you thought and felt in childhood.

Recovery from resentments IS attainable. Forgiveness for those who rejected you and for your own unloving behaviors that may have resulted is a gift that God is waiting and anxious to give to you.

Many people who feel rejection feel isolated and alone. They are sure that no one else could feel the depth of despair that they are feeling. It is difficult for many to identify why they have these overwhelming feelings. These damaged individuals have no idea that their pain comes from a source other than their present circumstances.

Popular psychology has focused on physical, sexual, and emotional abuse such as verbal putdowns, but it has not focused on the severely negative influence of rejection on a person's life. Many people who come to counseling say that they were never able to identify what their pain was until they understood rejection and how it grew from tiny seeds of resentment. Rejection is subjective. It's something you feel, not just a specific incident or circumstance. It's an atmosphere you live in, like polluted air, that over time lowers your resistance to bounce back when bad things happen to you. Rejection is the most powerful poison the devil has ever produced to insidiously attack your spiritual and emotional immune system. And then when you need immunity most—when you lose a job, your spouse criticizes, or your "friends" spread lies about you—you have no resistance, and the result is illness—spiritual, emotional, and many times physical.

If you have recognized some "seeds" of resentment that have been sown into your life, now is the time to uproot them. And in their place plant God's seeds of acceptance. Hold on to the truth that Christ was Himself "despised and rejected by men." (See Isa. 53.) He's been there; done that! And now He says to you, "Abide in Me, and I in you. As the branch cannot bear fruit of itself, unless it abides in the vine, neither can you, unless you abide in Me. . . . If you abide in Me, and My words abide in you, you will ask what you desire, and it shall be done for you. . . . As the Father loved me, I also have loved you; abide in My love. . . . These things I have spoken to you that My joy may remain in you, and that your joy may be full. . . . You did not choose Me, but I chose you and appointed you that you should go and bear fruit, and that your fruit should remain, that whatever you ask the Father in My name He may give you. . . . If the world hates you, you know that it hated Me before it hated you. . . . These things I have spoken to you, that you should not be made to stumble" (selected passages from John 15:4–16:1, NKJV).

It's time to stop listening to the rejecting voices of your past and listen carefully to the God who loves you unconditionally! Are you listening?

CHAPTER 9

When You're Hit With Emotional Abuse

"Verbal abuse is like a tape recorder
that never stops playing."
Gregory L. Jantz

"Sticks and stones may break my bones, but words will never hurt me. And when I die, you will cry, for all the names you've called me." It was just a childhood jingle repeated when other kids hurt our feelings with words or name-calling. It was another way of singing "Na, naaa, na-na, naaa" in the face of opposition. I (Nancy) heard it over and over again, and it got so that I was very good at saying it myself, even though we all knew the message was a lie.

It was a way to stop the pain of hurtful words, even if for just a moment. What else can a child say in response to hurled insults and taunting jeers. How does a sensitive child stop the wound of rejection from getting deeper? It was wishful thinking that perhaps if we said it often enough, by some stroke of magic we would be able to deflect the pain. But it never worked, and I carried the pain of rejection for years from the thoughtless words said to me during my childhood.

Gail was my dearest childhood chum. We were both minorities. She was Jewish. There were no other Jewish kids who rode our school bus. And I was fat. We were a good match for each other. One day the kids would tease her. The next day it was my turn to get abused. She was called a dirty Jew, and I was nicknamed "Fatso." We always sat together on the bus for moral support. We both felt alienated from the rest of our classmates and humiliated by their constant teasing. While the theology and the lifestyles of our families was greatly different, our pain knit us together in a bond of love and survival.

My family was more strict than hers and surrounded me with overprotective parameters. They allowed me little time for playing at her house and not much time for her to play at mine. They said they were afraid of her influence and the lack of supervision in her home.

But in each other's homes we found what we lacked in our own. When Gail came to my house, she received the warmth and affection she was denied at her home. When I went to hers, I was free from the overprotection of four adults (my parents and grandparents) at mine. It was there I could skinny dip in the bubbling brook in the woods behind her house or drink a soda or eat a mustard sandwich. (I can't believe we ate them!) It was there I learned to love Jewish food and had the freedom to fix it whenever we wanted. And it was at my home that she learned of the unconditional love of the Savior, whom my family served. I celebrated Hanukkah at her house, and she celebrated Christmas with me.

My parents, however, felt their own values were threatened as I grew closer and closer to a friend whose lifestyle was so different. But when they tried to separate us, they did not count on the bond that had grown between us, nor did they understand the psychological reason for it—the two of us against a hostile world.

The summer when Gail turned sixteen and got her driver's license, she drove her family car about one hundred miles to the camp meeting held by our church and stayed overnight in our tent. Her coming was a great surprise to all of us. She arrived on the campgrounds while I was in a meeting, snuck in, and slipped into the seat beside me. She went to work with me on the campgrounds and accompanied me to every meeting, where she sang the songs and bowed in prayer just as if she was one of us.

My parents were baffled by this event and still did not understand the reason for the intensity of the bond of misery we shared. Misery likes company!

All children at times suffer from the thoughtless words of others that carry the pain of emotional abuse. Too many suffer from verbal abuse at home, or as in the case of Gail, from emotional neglect. I, at least, was fortunate enough to have the emotional cushion of a friend during the years I felt rejected by my classmates.

What is emotional or verbal abuse? It is any word said that does not uplift or edify. It could also be the hurtful lack of hearing words of affirmation. With that broad definition, who is there then, who has never been emotionally abused?

Why are hurtful words so destructive? In his book entitled *Healing the Scars of Emotional Abuse,* Gregory L. Jantz outlines the answer to this question. He says that emotional abuse "is damaging because it outlives its own life span. Not only does it damage a person's self-esteem at the time it is done, but it also sets up a life-pattern that daily assaults the inner-being" (31).

Since we as humans pivot on our self-worth and feel we are a success or a failure based on the view we have of ourselves, emotional abuse can set us onto a merry-go-round that spins to the music of the insults we've heard. Its speed and destructive intensity increases with each subsequent demeaning word that is hurled our way.

Jantz further explains that *emotional abuse robs victims*

of a sense of security and value. Life has order to it, and human beings need that order. They need to know what to expect. It helps them feel safe and secure and have a sense of control. The victim of emotional abuse usually cannot predict the time, place, or intensity of future abuse. The abuse is dependent upon the mood of the perpetrator. For the child, life is as uncertain as the parent's mood. If Mother wakes up happy, then perhaps the child can get off to school without being hit by hurtful words. But if Mother is grouchy, regardless of what the child does, there is a good chance the child will get criticized or yelled at. It's frightening when no amount of performance can seem to shut it down. If one cannot be successful at achieving the control required that would stop the putdowns, then the victim considers the perpetrator to be in total control of his or her own emotions and responses—dangling the victim like a puppet on a string.

Emotional abuse creates in its victims a sense of fear—that there are no safe moments when the abuse will not occur, no right words to prevent the attack or to use as a comeback to stop the abuser. Especially for a child, there is no closure, no resolve, and no way to settle the matter without receiving the damage.

Since fear is a paralytic agent, its victim feels helpless to stop the trauma. It's like being in a nightmare where you are trying desperately to run, but your legs won't move. Therefore, you stand motionless, unable to escape from the stinging words or intimidating looks. The implied messages of emotional abuse pack a similar life-threatening punch to a loaded gun. Words may not kill the body, but they have the power to destroy the spirit.

Guilt is another result of emotional abuse. The damaging feelings of guilt, which disintegrate into destructive feelings of shame, render the victim hopeless of ever becoming acceptable and worthwhile. Guilt gives us the message that we have done a wrong thing or neglected a right one. Shame goes beyond guilt to the deeper level of thinking and feeling that we are wrong. Shame sets us up to feel incorrigible, without hope of change or improvement. It is clear why Satan would want us to live in shame. He would then have little to battle, because we would refuse to fight him. When one knows he or she will lose, why fight? Wouldn't it be less effort to just give up?

Anger is another reason why emotional abuse is so damaging. Experiences of injustice leave the victim filled with rage and fearful of expressing it. This bottled life-destroying emotion has the potential to cause physical, emotional, and sexual dysfunctions within the life of its captive. This rage increases to a fevered pitch as day after day the damage is increased by rekindling the original fire every time a new assault is mounted. In other words, current abuse causes all the old abuse to resurface, which makes the pain even more intensive.

David's untimely and tragic death is a perfect example of the destructive rage created by emotional abuse. He was the middle child in the family, sandwiched between an older sister and a younger brother. As the oldest son, he was expected to carry adult responsibility, and when he didn't— and for no reason at all—he received severe physical and emotional abuse at the hand of his father.

We have witnessed David being kicked down an entire flight of stairs with his father screaming obscenities and insults all the way down. As a child, David witnessed the often repeated beatings perpetrated upon his mother by this brutish man and had felt abandoned by the mother, whose bruised and battered state prevented her from getting up off the couch to cook, wash clothes, or perform necessary routine tasks.

David had watched in horror as his incested sister married a fellow who would treat her the way his mom had been treated for twenty-four years. And he was relieved when after a year of beatings Laurie left her persecutor, only to watch her marry again. This time she married a "good" guy, one who would not hurt her, but the moment of truth came about six years later, when the one beating she received in this marriage nearly took her life. He had stood by her as she divorced husband number two, and she received full custody of their children. Why would she then be driven to another destructive live-in relationship? Could she not live without a man?

David had been the one who discovered the lifeless body of his younger brother hanging from a flagpole he'd climbed; who summoned every possible piece of rescue equipment to bring Mark down, hoping that he could be revived. It was David who had the job of telling Ma that her youngest child had committed suicide. Why? Because he hated himself for being just like Dad and hitting his girlfriend on a date that evening. David had watched his mother's spirit die at that funeral, blaming herself for not being a "good enough" mother who could have prevented this senseless loss.

David had been there to hold his mother's hand and comfort her when the doctors announced her diagnosis: breast cancer. Prognosis: poor. Six months to live. He wondered, "Were all of the blows that Dad directed at Mom's breasts the cause of this impending loss?"

He was there when we were—at her bedside in the hospice unit where she had gone to die. The sight of her sickened his stomach but more so to his heart, intensifying the rage that had been building since infancy—rage for the man he felt was responsible for all the garbage in their lives, including his own. Dad's insulting words still rang in his ears, because he continued in the only job he thought he could do—working for his father at the garage-door business. Fortunately, Dad was not present every day, because he was living in another state with the woman he had divorced Mom to marry. While the weekly pain intensified over the phone, the old insults and putdowns rang loudly in his ears during each waking moment. He had come to realize that Dad was still controlling him through the painful and persistent recall of the old junk.

David hated his father! We all knew it, and nobody faulted him for it. We knew that the hate would ultimately destroy him, and we told him so. We begged and pleaded for him to get some professional help so that he could let go of this controlling emotion. But David would not; perhaps he thought himself unworthy of relief. Instead, he endured the torture of his mother's death and funeral and kept hidden deep inside him the volatile rage that controlled his every breath.

On a hot and steamy summer day, David's decomposing body was discovered. The stench of death had oozed out of his house and into the neighborhood, prompting a neighbor to summon the police. We are told that it was a gruesome sight and have no desire to know more.

The coroner ruled out drugs, alcohol, and foul play and pronounced the cause of death as a massive heart attack. David's heart had literally exploded from the stress of loss, coupled with the life-threatening emotions of hatred and rage. Finally the tapes of insulting and demeaning putdowns directed at him and his loved ones by a totally out of control father had ceased their playing.

The pain of emotional abuse is so damaging because the tapes play on and on and control the decisions of the victim until intervention comes to break the tape or the recorder dies.

You may wonder what kind of a brute would do such despicable things to his family. How had Satan so taken control of this father's life as to prompt him to create such havoc in the lives of his children and brutalize his partner for a quarter of a century?

David's father was also a victim. He had been raised in a very violent home by a father who was totally out of control. A man who brutalized his wife, even in the company of others, and whose self-hate was perpetrated on his entire family. There were several sons in the family, and Ben (David's father) was definitely not the favorite.

One Thanksgiving, inlaws and extended family were together at the home of David's grandparents. Twenty or more people sat around a huge table. At one point in the meal, the grandfather noticed that his wife had spilled a drop of gravy on her bosom. He got up from his seat and went into the kitchen for a wet dishrag and returned to the table, and with his fist in the dishrag he began to beat her breast, screaming obscenities at her because she had spilled the gravy. The entire family witnessed the event, and for the first time a window of understanding was created about the origin of their son Ben's brutish behavior.

In the minds of those sitting around the table were judgments and criticisms of what they had just seen. The human mind needs completion. It needs an answer, and if one is not presented to us, we manufacture our own. There were probably as many judgments as there were people at the table. Everyone differs in temperament, life experiences, education, etc., and because our foundations vary widely, no one's behavioral structure will be identical to anothers. We should carefully take all this into account before judging or criticizing what we do not understand or approve of in others.

We have no right to sit on the judge's bench when we have not listened to all the evidence. And when we think we know all the evidence, we usually know only a fraction.

While it has been the family's habit to judge David's father, Ben, so harshly and to reject him from family gatherings and special events, our responses may have been greatly different had we known the whole truth about his family of origin. This, however, does not excuse the abusive behavior of David's father, but it does supply the reason. If Grandfather would treat his wife as he did with many guests seated around his table, what must he have done to her and the children with no witnesses around?

We could trace David's lineage as far back as records are kept, and if we went back far enough, we would end up at the Garden of Eden. It was there that Satan launched his first attack on our original parents, whose damage has then poisoned their children and ours.

Should we just shrug our shoulders and say, "What can we do? How can you possibly stop Satan's army of destroyers?" We can do it one step at a time, and the process begins in our own minds and yours. It takes an awareness of the forces against us, and it takes trust in the omnipotence of God, whose power far exceeds that of His enemy. It takes a willingness to say "I cannot. But you can, Lord." It takes complete surrender, openness, and vulnerability. It takes a willingness to say "I'm guilty. The pain I carry may not be my responsibility, but my behavior's are my responsibility, because they end up damaging myself and those around me. I recognize that all the power of heaven is available to me to guide me out of captivity to Satan and into the freedom found in Jesus Christ. I must make the choice."

David suffered more than emotional abuse. All forms of abuse strike damaging blows to our emotions. In physical abuse, the victim feels helpless, worthless, and discarded. These are emotions, so we could say, then, that physical abuse produces emotional abuse. The same is true with sexual abuse, in which the most devastating result is a loss of a sense of self. The victim ends up confused about worth and value, identity, position in life, and these produce behaviors that further damage the delicate feelings of a victim.

The message received by the victim is the key to the damage. Most forms of abuse project a very loud message that attacks self-identity and self-worth. These messages, spoken or unspoken, are designed to shame, to devalue, and to belittle, but the real intent is to get control of the victim. If these are given by a person from whom the victim needs love and direction, they produce a more devastating result. If they are given by previously trusted individuals, they carry more weight. Because the abused believes the abuser, the abusive words and actions become an established part of a person's belief system on which all future decisions are based.

Not all abusers are aware of their intent and the real damage they are doing to another. Some are simply living out what they have been exposed to and victimized by, and others know well that what they are doing is following their own plan to control another person. Just like David's father, many are acting out what has been done to them and what seems to be the normal thing to do. Abuse has become a habit; a way of life.

Being rewounded time after time finally sets in cement a belief system about worth and value. It's out of that belief system that abused individuals will live for the remainder of their lives if intervention does not take place. Victims repeatedly seek out those who reabuse them and sabotage healthy relationships. They may not like the words said or the things done to them, but the feelings these damages create within them have become their identity. If they found a friend who would not abuse them, they would leave that person because they are uncomfortable in the safety zone of love, protection, and care.

Recently while speaking to a group of women from a battered women's shelter, I (Nancy) asked the women to close their eyes. "Think back in time to when you had a boyfriend who was whole and healthy, who treated you in a loving and respectful manner. Recall how you felt when you were with him. What specifically did you do to end that relationship?"

I watched them intensely, looking for a facial or an emotional response to the memory I had evoked. A few cried; others nodded their head in agreement. Then I said to them, "On the count of three, say his name out loud." There was not a silent voice in the group. One woman spoke out, "This is totally incredible. I thought I was the only stupid one in the bunch. But everybody around this table knew exactly what person they had dumped to marry someone who would abuse them the way they had been abused before."

The sad truth became very evident that day: That abused women will choose abusive men in order to maintain their misinformed identity. What is so amazing here is that for lack of knowledge the spirits of these women were perishing.

As we discussed around the table, the women brought to my attention their own behaviors that demonstrated their childhood emotional abuse. These included the following, and each relates to one of Erik Erikson's tasks of emotional development: Trust, autonomy, initiative, industry, identity, and intimacy.

- *Low self-worth* is an attack on the ability to trust self or others, which should have been developed during the first eighteen months of life. Over time abusers lower the self-worth of their victims and in so doing are able to shackle the victims to themselves by an invisible chain of fear and self-doubt. The message received is "I need my abuser. I cannot trust myself. I cannot make it on my own."

- *Lack of self-confidence* is an attack on one's decision-making ability—or one's autonomy. The basic foundation for autonomy comes between eighteen months to three years of age. The ability to govern one's life is surrendered to the abuser even though the decisions they make often go against what the victim feels is right or appropriate.

- *Workaholism or perfectionism, and the flip side, which is a lack of drive or courage to try.* This is an attack on the development of initiative, which is the third level of Erik Erikson's developmental tasks, which comes during the preschool years of three to six. Those who have been abused will endeavor to hide or protect the truth by overcompensating into long hours of work with a need to do every task to perfection. Or they give up and don't even try.

- *Under-achievement and a sense of failure* are the results of the internal hopelessness created by emotional abuse. Many feel that since they have never achieved anything, completing a project or performing to another's satisfaction is impossible. They are both incapable and unworthy of success and will do whatever they need to do to prevent themselves from reaching their potential. This is an attack on the developmental task of industry that we hope to see in children during the early school years of six to twelve.

- *Inability to establish personhood, healthy sexuality, meaningful friendships, and adult responsibilities.* Erik Erikson labels the developmental task that earmarks the teen years, identity. It is during this time that teens must establish who they are as separate from their families. The hormonal and physical changes during these years complicates the ease of passing from childhood to adulthood. The abused have a greater struggle because adulthood requires responsibility and achievement. If they feel worthless, inadequate, and fearful of change, they will remain enmeshed with family or with whomever will orchestrate or control their lives for them. That's why, over and over again, abused women choose controlling men. That's why teens will submit to the sexual demands placed on them and conform to the social pressures of irresponsible peers.

- *Isolation, loneliness and alienation, or a drivenness toward sexual connection that results in instant relationships that go from the "bar" to the bedroom.* Abused individuals crave intimacy, which is the developmental task of young adults from eighteen to thirty-five years of age, but they don't know how to establish it. Because of their damage, they confuse the word *intimacy* with the word *sex*. That's why the above behaviors look so different from each other. It is important to understand that out of abuse come behaviors that can be at either end of the pendulum swing or at any point in between. Whether persons swing to the left or the right depends on the nature of their abuse and their own innate characteristics. Many victims feel isolated while with another person in a crowded room; others feel they must sexually conquer everyone they meet. Satan has confused our view of intimacy.

True intimacy is the connecting of mind with mind. In a healthy relationship sexuality is not a necessary ingredient, but in a marriage it becomes the physical expression of the couple's emotional connection and the symbol of lifetime one-flesh commitment.

Two friends of the same sex can be intimate with each other without arousing sexual feelings. Take, for example, how I (Nancy) have worked with our co-author, Kay, in the development of this book. We had met several times before but with no opportunity for personal sharing of any kind. In the quiet of Kay's Tennessee mountain home, we sat in two recliners facing each other, and we began the discussion of what Ron and I had in mind for this book. And something clicked!

As we wrote the content, we felt a freedom to share with each other personal history that we may have never shared with others, other than our spouses. That sense of ease and comfortableness between Kay and me is what God designed should be between friends willing to lay down their lives for the other. It is the joy of sharing between a husband and a wife. It is the relationship He desires to have with us as His beloved children. *True intimacy is a oneness without fear of retribution or betrayal.* It contains a deep sharing of soul without fear of judgment or criticism.

The ability to be intimate is dependent on specific building blocks that must be acquired during the different developmental stages of a child's life. For example, in the very first stage, the nude, wet baby is placed on the mother's abdomen and nuzzles at her breast. This intimacy forms the basis for a child for what will be building throughout the years, climaxing with the sexual intimacy with a marital partner.

As intimacy is being developed in teenage years, it embraces all the previous experiences, both positive and negative, and each plays a part in the teen's and future adult's ability or inability to experience true intimacy with another.

Emotional abuse distorts God's design for intimacy. It demands submission; the surrendering of personhood into the prison of meeting the demands or fulfilling the needs of another. It is about making another person wrong while always maintaining the status of rightness. Even truth is received with a "well, not necessarily" so that others are always in a "no win" situation.

A person cannot last long in a relationship where being wrong is a regular component. The need to be right forfeits intimacy. The need to distance in order to capture a certain amount of worth and value becomes a driving force to the one who has been emotionally abused.

Emotional abuse tells the hurting ones the repetitious lie that they are worthless and holds before them Satan's counterfeit for intimacy-illicit sex. That's why today's movies, TV programs, soaps, romance novels, magazines, and billboards are so enticing to hurting people. They speak to the need for connection but offer the counterfeit of a momentary thrill. Each sexual conquest only reaffirms what the abused already know, that they have no worth or value outside of sexual performance. Each hit of emotional abuse increases the reservoir of rejection.

But this is fixable! With God nothing is impossible (see Mark 10:27). If you become teachable and willing to examine yourself, past and present, God's grace (His unmerited divine assistance) will assist you to empty your reservoir of resentment and fill it with His acceptance.

We have always read that Jesus was despised and rejected—a man of sorrows and acquainted with grief. (See Isa. 53:3.) It was only when reading further in a commentary about His early life that we understood the extent of His rejection—including His own family and His hometown neighbors. We can just imagine the emotional sticks and stones that were thrown His way. We can hear angry playmates chanting "Na, naaa, nana, naaa! You don't have a daddy!" We hear His jealous siblings accusing, "You think you're a goody, goody. But you're just kissing up to make brownie points with the folks." We overhear the insensitive grown-ups whisper as He passes, "There goes Mary's illegitimate son. Can you imagine anyone coming up with such a crazy story as to be impregnated by God! Ha! Ha!"

How must Jesus have felt? It helps us feel better just to know that He endured everything we have ever been asked to endure. "For we do not have a High Priest who cannot sympathize with our weaknesses, but was in all points tempted as we are, yet without sin" (Heb. 4:15, NKJV).

If you are the victim of emotional abuse, take hope in this wonderful promise from your loving Father in heaven:

> *"You shall be called by a new name,*
> *Which the mouth of the Lord will name.*
> *You shall also be a crown of glory*
> *In the hand of the Lord,*
> *And a royal diadem*
> *In the hand of your God.*
> *You shall no longer be termed forsaken . . .*
> *For the Lord delights in you. . . .*
> *So shall your God rejoice over you."*
> *Isaiah 62:2-5, NKJV*

CHAPTER 10

Who Am I? Innocent Child or Passionate Adult

"Sexual abuse is the final blow
that sabotages the soul in a climactic betrayal,
mocking the enjoyment of relationship
and pouring contempt on the thrill of passion."
Dan B. Allender

In the 1960's, an autobiography was published that shocked mainstream America. It was written by a woman we know as Sybil who had endured unbelievable sexual abuse. Her damage wreaked havoc upon her life until in desperation she sought the help of a psychiatrist. In the process of recovery, Sybil acted out a bizarre array of more than fifteen different personalities. Sybil's story, purchased by Hollywood, helped us to become aware of a psychotic illness known as Multiple Personality Disorder (MPD).

In viewing the film, one begins to comprehend the chaos such an illness creates in the lives and relationships of its victims. In Sybil's case, she had fractured into alternate "others" to withstand the severe physical, psychological, and sexual pain experienced in early childhood. The conscious memory of her abuse had been filed away in her inaccessible subconscious mind. Yet the trauma of those early events orchestrated the fracturing of self and fostered her inability to understand what was happening to her.

The result was that Sybil found her life in shambles and her relationships with others floundering and dying. What she desperately needed—love and acceptance—she couldn't grab hold of because she couldn't trust herself. Her sense of personhood had been trampled and smashed. Her various personalities, appearing upon the scene as if out of nowhere, simply underscored the hopelessness of her life.

Sybil's sexual abuse was perpetrated by the one who should have nurtured her the most—her mother. When the loving connection that should be present between parent and child is missing, the resulting experience is rejection—feelings of not belonging, being an outsider, having no value, and being unimportant. It is also true that the most nurturing parent has the potential to create the most severe damage. When a parent on one hand shows love and adoration and on the other humiliates and violates, the mixed messages create psychological chaos in the child.

In essence, all sexual abuse produces feelings of rejection in the victim. Dr. Dan B. Allender in his classic book *The Wounded Heart* describes sexual abuse as a betrayal, "A disregard or harm done to the dignity of another as a result of one's commitment to find life apart from God." The fact is, with God there is always acceptance; without Him, there is nothing but rejection.

Allender further states that sexual abuse has three levels. "The failure of the family to nourish the child prior to the abuse, the traitorous act of the perpetrator, and the lack of protection offered by the nonoffending parent(s)" (130).

Rejection is evident at each level. The first level is a nonnourishing family environment. When basic needs of a child are unmet, the child interprets that omission as rejection. On the second level, by forcing the child into an adult role, the child is rejected as an innocent nonsexual child. And on the third level, the lack of protection by the family gives a clear message that the child is not worthy of the kind of care and concern that could have prevented the abuse, or if not prevented it, at least would not have swept it under the rug in order to protect the family name or perpetrator. Children feel rejected when they think others are more important than they are.

When children feel rejection, an avalanche of destructive feelings and behaviors come crashing down on them: poor self-worth, fear, anxiety, guilt, depression, anger, hostility, and aggression.

The fact is, children (having God's built-in software that contains the laws for the healthy functioning of mind and body) are not prepared for the introduction of sexuality. Not until the anatomy and physiology of the body is mature enough to handle sexual behaviors is the mind able to comprehend the depth and meaning of sexual intimacy. Most estimate that sexual maturity (not the capacity to reproduce) happens about the age of eighteen. God's laws in the mind require that sex takes place within the commitment of marital vows, and any sexual behaviors outside of that bond are in direct opposition to the law, creating internal confusion and guilt. In childhood sexual abuse, the value of the child is placed on the sexual services the child supplies. Sexual abuse switches the child's self-worth from who the child is to what the child does.

For the child, sexual abuse often creates physical as well as psychological pain, sometimes so severe that the only way the mind and body can handle it is to disassociate; to divide oneself so that the pain cannot be felt. Many adults, whose history includes repeated sexual abuse, testify that they "watched their own abuse happening from another spot in the room." This often creates the foundation of MPD and/or the necessity to shut off feelings when another situation later in life threatens physical or emotional safety.

Abused children, in addition to the physical and psychological pain they endure, often live under the threat that if the truth is told, they will be killed. These little ones find no place to run for safety, because the very ones who should protect them are either guilty of the damage or the child has been told that if the child tells, their mother or father will also be killed. This forces abused children into invisible torture chambers; locked inside prisons of lies and "dirty little secrets." These victims are isolated from those who should or could listen, comfort, and rescue.

If there is no safe place for abused children to tell what has happened to them, they hold onto the pain and relive it again and again, exaggerating the damage. *If there was a safe place for children to share what had happened to them and caring and concerned individuals who would listen, convince them that they are not at fault, validate them, and take the necessary steps to stop the abuse and allow the perpetrator to suffer the legal consequences, the pain's impact and the emotional confusion could be greatly lessened.*

Instead, many parents sabotage the healing process by unintentionally placing the blame on the child by keeping the secret in order to protect the family's name, the perpetrator, or even a church organization. The load of guilt that rightfully belongs on others is then borne alone by the victim. Abused children begin to fear all others who might have the potential to reinflict similar damage upon them. It is all too common that they withdraw into a world of their own.

The neediness of children who do not have whole, healthy, and protective parents is misinterpreted by some and used by others as the opening they are looking for to reabuse them. Children who have been damaged early in life seem to attract with alluring magnetism those who will reabuse them. Then because their boundaries have been destroyed or severely damaged, they are vulnerable to the advances or attacks of others.

Kristy was the victim of incest from the cradle to her midteens. Her only memories of childhood were of the abuse she suffered at the hands of her father. She was raped twice in her teenage years, married twice to men who physically, emotionally, and sexually abused her, and then a third time to a man who placed the stability of their marriage and his commitment to it on her willingness to meet his sexual addiction.

Kristy began to lose her grip on reality about the time her boss forced her into sexual behaviors with him in order for her to maintain her employment. Since Kristy had no boundaries, because they had been smashed in her toddler years by an ignorant father, she was not able to say No. She did not think that she had the right to refuse; that right had been stripped from her. Simultaneously her husband put sexual demands on her that she could not handle. She began to believe that her life was not worth living. The pressure was too much! Five times she cried out for help in the only way she knew how, by making flubbed attempts at suicide. Still the pressure continued from her husband, who felt that she used the history of her incest as an excuse to not be as sexual as he wanted her to be in the marital bed.

The sad thing is that Kristy's story of early sexual abuse is not an isolated one. Dr. Lloyd deMause, president of the International Psychohistorical Association, reported in a paper he presented in 1994 to the American Psychiatric Association, "I have concluded that the real sexual abuse rate for America is 60% for girls and 45% for boys, about half directly incestuous."

Other Western nations have made fewer careful studies. A recent Canadian study by Gallup of 2,000 adults has produced incidence rates almost exactly the same as those found in the United States. Latin American family sexual activity—particularly wide-spread pederasty as part of macho sexuality—is considered even more widespread. In England, a recent BBC "ChildWatch" program asked its female listeners—a large though admittedly biased sample—if they remembered sexual molestation, and, of the 2,530 replies analyzed, 83% remembered someone touching their genitals, 62% recalling actual intercourse. In Germany, the Institute fuer Kindheit has recently concluded a survey asking West Berlin school children about their sexual experiences, and 80% reported having been molested. Outside the West, the sexual molestation of children is a routine practice in most families. Childhood in India begins, according to observers, with the child being regularly masturbated by the mother, the girl "to make her sleep well," the boy "to make him manly." The child sleeps in the family bed, witnesses and most likely takes part in sexual intercourse between the parents. The child is often "borrowed" to sleep with other members of the extended household, leading to the Indian proverb that "For a girl to be a virgin at ten years old, she must have neither brothers, nor cousin, or father." (Unpublished manuscript, *History of Child Abuse,* available from The International Psycho-historical Association, at 140 Riverside Drive, New York, New York, 10024.)

Dr. deMause goes on to report that China, Japan, and other Far East and Near East countries have similar abusive practices. One of the most shocking practices he described was a ritual among Arab families where the mutilation of female genitalia by a clitoridectomy and the removal of the labia ended the ability of the girl to ever again feel sexual pleasure. Unbelievably, this cruelty is performed by other women in revenge, because their husbands prefer sex with little girls!

Young children who are sexually abused live in fear of a reoccurrence of abuse, which could happen at any time and any place. But this fear, rather than reducing the chance of avoiding the fearful situation in the future, increases it. In other words, the fearing of sexual abuse almost always sets the victim up to receive it. This is opposite to the healthy use of fear, which causes one to fight or flee. Instead, sexual abuse produces paralyzing fear that prevents the victim from just saying No. Boundaries are so smashed that the victim doesn't even know she or he has the right to refuse.

Let's return to Kristy's story to illustrate this. Abused as a child and fearing more abuse, she fell victim to the advances of every man in her life because she was so needy. The male figure in her life in her character-forming years, who should have been a whole, healthy daddy, was instead a desperately damaged abuser. And so, having been invalidated and untreasured by her daddy as a little girl, she longed for a man who would fill her childhood needs for nurturing, warmth, and affection. Instead, she was driven to seek men just like Daddy because that was all she knew. Her neediness screamed so loudly that she automatically reverted to what was "normal" for her and endured more sexual abuse in order to get her needs met.

Healthy fear is a result of receiving all the childhood emotional needs necessary to have a sense of self that enables growing children to set healthy boundaries for their own safety. Sexual abuse removes one's sense of self, and the child remains enmeshed with the abuser, feeling responsible to meet all the abuser's needs. The abused child is saddled with a love/hate relationship. The law of the mind is to "honor your father," and so the abused child who has become an adult will obey the law by being attracted to men like the father and as a result is constantly reabused.

Some women are so fearful of their fathers that they will look for men who are extremely safe; men from whom they have received no sexual demands or men whom they perceive have expressed no sexual desire for them. In either case, marrying like Daddy or entirely different from Daddy, the girl is reabused in the marriage. How? Either like Kristy, she is constantly being reabused by a sexually driven man or having learned in childhood that she was only valuable for the sexual favors she could give, she is emotionally and sexually deprived by a man who rejects and avoids her sexually. She reasons, "If my husband doesn't desire me sexually, I am worthless. I have no value!"

It might be well to note that we marry people of similar levels of damage. The sexually driven or addicted man has his own damage in childhood, which produces his drivenness. And the man who avoids sexuality has his own childhood baggage that shuts down his ability to connect with a woman in a healthy emotional and sexual way.

Vicky's story illustrates this point. Vicky was just past toddler stage when she began wandering off to the safety of the little white church down the street from her house. What was happening to her at home was a mystery. She knew she hurt but had no idea this physical pain would result in emotional pain that she would carry for years to come. There beneath a pew in the quiet of the sanctuary she clutched her dolly and created an imaginary family where there was no screaming and hollering, no angry outbursts, no violation of her personhood, and no midnight visits to her bed by a drunken father.

Vicky was one of eleven children, the second to the youngest. Her family lived in poverty, with father drinking away large portions of his meager income. Mother worked inside their tiny hovel trying to keep it clean for her brood and outside the home to supplement the income of her laborer husband.

Often the care of the younger children fell to the older daughters, who resented the intrusion of the little waif into their teenage lives. The older girls had been physically abused by their father and had witnessed their mother being physically abused by him as well. Other men had come to their home when Father was at work, and Mother had entertained them, but the children did not understand the full impact of the adulterous affairs.

Vicky became the last of her father's incest victims, beginning at about age three, and recalls him approaching her as she lay on her little rollaway bed. The smell of the beer oozing from his body and the feel of his whiskers needling her delicate face was accompanied by painful intrusion into her tiny body. As a result of her abuse, Vicky regularly wet her bed. Each morning when her sister came to make it, if the sheets were wet, she would grab Vicky's blond hair and rub her face in the soiled sheets as if training a puppy. She would then throw her tiny body onto the bed and fold it up with Vicky locked inside. There she would stay for several hours before being released by some other family member. Other times she was locked out of the house; left for hours in the cold.

The first time Vicky spoke of her painful childhood, she spoke only of physical abuse. Her memory of sexual abuse did not return until some time later when she was ready to receive the truth, had a nurturing support system, and enough trust in God to rely on Him to carry her through.

The morning after the last memory returned, she phoned her oldest sister for a reality check. She learned that in addition to incest from her father, she had also been used by her older brothers, their friends, and even other men in the family.

Vicky's process of healing began when she acknowledged the truth and was willing to plunge headlong into a process to remove the painful emotion from the memories of her past. Several months later she began to look at her husband with new eyes. Suddenly it dawned on her why she had felt so isolated in her marriage; Dave must also have been abused.

Gently she began to ask questions, but he had few answers. One afternoon while journaling, Vicky was struck by a new possibility. "Could it be that Dave, too, was a victim of incest?" She remembered how shortly after their wedding she found Dave's mother washing his back as he soaked in the bathtub. Vicky was paralyzed. Her rage hit ten and exploded later when they were alone. "Don't you ever allow that woman to see you naked again. She had you as a child, but now you are mine!"

Then the picture of her honeymoon night flashed across her mind. Dave had gotten a room with twin beds! She remembers lying in one of the beds while he was in the shower, wondering what choice he would make. He came out of the shower in his PJs and stood there staring from one bed to the other. She remained silent. Finally he climbed into the other twin bed. She lay there for a while vacillating between anger, rejection, and sadness—and quietly the tears soaked her pillow. She silently screamed, "Why did every other man in my life want to paw all over me and the one I love, with a marriage license, doesn't even want to touch me? I don't understand."

At the time of this new insight about the possibility of Dave being abused, Vicky and Dave had been married nineteen years. She mused, "Where did our children ever come from? Our sexual encounters have been so scarce they must have been immaculately conceived!"

Then the thought came to her. "He is a man. So where is he getting his sexual needs met?" She pondered, "He wouldn't step outside our marriage? Not Dave! Would he?" Shortly afterward she discovered him pleasuring himself and realized that masturbation was the way he had chosen!

This revelation devastated her. "Why?" she agonized to him. "Am I so ugly that you can't stand me? Could doing that really be more fulfilling than enjoying me?"

Dave was silent. But the shock of having his ugly secret discovered and seeing the unbelievable pain it caused the woman he adored forced him to dig into his own past. Together they discovered abuses he had carried subconsciously. And together they began the process of demolishing the past and rebuilding the future.

You might question, Why would a person turn to masturbation rather than enjoying a willing marital partner? In our counseling experience we have observed that the law of mind/

body relationships says that when a man receives a woman's emotional load, his body often requires a sexual expression.

In Dave's search he discovered he had been carrying emotional baggage which his mother, out of her marital neediness, began to pile on him in early childhood. But God's law in the mind says that you may not be sexual with your mother, so he turned to self-gratification. When Dave recognized the truth of his past, he was not only willing, but anxious, to lay down his mother's baggage and connect with his wife.

Molestation differs from incest in that the perpetrator is not a family member. He or she may be a friend of the family, a babysitter, a neighbor, or a perfect stranger who interacts with a child in a sexual manner creating fear. This molestation can be a look, words, inappropriate touch, or penetration.

June was in first grade. One day on her way back to school from lunch break, a strange car pulled up beside her. A man she did not know offered her a candy bar and a ride back to the school. Innocently, she accepted. The events of the next hour became the foundation for confusion, fear, and guilt that would last into her forties. The stranger took her to a wooded area. There he exposed his genitals, forced her to touch, and when he was satisfied, drove her back to the school. When she walked into the classroom, her teacher indignantly asked her, "Well, young lady, where do you think you've been?"

June had no answer. How does a six-year-old describe what has just happened to her when she is paralyzed with fear and doesn't have the vocabulary to explain?

Her lack of response created rage within the teacher, who considered her silence as insolence. Placing a dunce cap on her head, the teacher sat June in front of the class for the rest of the day.

June had just been punished for the abuse she had just suffered, and the child-mind interpretation was that the whole event was her fault. Unfortunately, home was not a safe place either, and so she never shared with anyone the truth about what happened that day.

In her early forties, June approached me (Nancy) following a seminar. "What's wrong with me?" she asked. Unwilling to give me the benefit of her history or symptoms, she insisted I diagnose her problem by observation. Finally removing her glasses, she asked disgustedly. "Can't you tell; can't you see that I don't have any eyebrows and eyelashes?"

In the next few moments we ruled out a physical disease, and then I asked, "At what age were you first sexually abused?"

June had no idea that the secret that she had never told had caused her a lifetime of pain; that the anxiety she felt stemmed way back to the first incident of sexual abuse when she was six. The habit of plucking out her eyelashes and eyebrows stemmed from the anxiety and fear she felt, wondering when it would happen again.

Many times the memory of molestation lies dormant until some moment in the intimacy of the marital bed a stimulus triggers the repressed memory of pain and humiliation. When that memory surfaces, the mate in the bed is imagined to be the molester. Frozen with fear, the victim recalls the past and experiences anxiety about the future.

(Nancy) I vividly recall the moment when the body responses I had been feeling blended with a newly returned memory. How does a wife explain to her husband that her stiffened body is responding to the old man across the street who had taken advantage of her vulnerability when she was just a little girl? The terror I felt at the moment was without words. There was no way to tell Ron. If I told the truth, I feared I would be discarded like yesterday's rubbish. I predicted that he would disbelieve my story and once again I would be rejected. For fifteen years I lived with the conscious memory of what had happened but could not share my secret. The consequences of this truth were too frightening to me. Over and over again Ron and I would discuss our sexuality, and each discussion would send me into deeper agony. I was more and more convinced that I was at fault for Ron's dissatisfaction with our sexual relationship.

About two years before I shared my history with Ron, we had become aware of the impact of childhood damage on adult thinking, feeling, and behaving. When Ron finally came to admit his sexual drivenness, which stemmed from his childhood damage, I summoned the courage to share my own damage. Perhaps this time I wouldn't be blamed for everything he thought was wrong with our sexual relationship.

(Ron) I had to learn academically how sexual damage effects a man and a marital relationship before I was willing to admit that anything was wrong with me. Since men look outside of themselves for the blame for all relational problems, I had a handy target in Nancy. I was convinced that if she would only . . . Then the sexual part of our marriage would be bliss. Remember, I was a rejected child and had no idea that lack of touch expresses itself in behaviors that are similar to those of sexual abuse. I also did not recognize the impact of the memory of my boys'-club experience when I was four or five. In the club where I was learning to swim, no one, including the instructors, were allowed to wear swimming suits in the pool. Vividly I remember being called out of the pool by the whistle and heading for the locker room. Beyond the locker-room door, everything is black, but my rage goes off the scale. Something happened in that locker room, just what, I don't know. But I do know that some of the cruelest abuse takes place in locker rooms.

When I was nine, an older teen in my neighborhood molested me. That experience, painful, humiliating, and disgusting to me, forced me to ask the question, "What is feminine about me that would make a man desire me?" That question repeated over and over in the mind sets a boy to attempt to prove his masculinity through multiple sexual conquests of women for a lifetime. Enough is never enough. As long as the doubt remains, there must be another conquest. I looked for any sign from a woman that she had an interest in me; even the slightest smile from her said to me that I might be sexually desirable.

I was so empty, so rejected, so needy, so desirous of acceptance, that I looked everywhere to have my need to be touched satisfied. Early exposure to pornography, masturbation, peep shows, and massage parlors, all became contributing agents to fill the void in my life left by the lack of a mother's touch and the question of my manhood. I was so vulnerable at that point that if I would have had a loving and accepting male who initiated sexual contact, my heterosexual identity may have been lost. It was only when I came to understand my rejection, and began the process to eliminate my negative emotions regarding it, that my drivenness began to diminish.

Why is sexual damage so prevalent? Why spend an entire chapter looking at such seemingly gross abuse?

Remember that Satan has an agenda, and his agenda is to destroy. Sexual damage strikes at the core of people's identity. It sabotages their sense of worth and value. It robs them of even the physical feelings of self. It gives the loud message that "I am worthy only of being used and abused and of never connecting in an intimate emotional relationship."

Shocking statistics report that the majority of women who prostitute themselves were childhood victims of incest. Because of an unfulfilled need for a whole and healthy father, these abused women sexually search for a lifetime for a man who will be the daddy they never had and desperately needed. Sadly enough, these women learn all too soon that the men who choose to pay them for sexual services are not the caliber to "father" them in a healthy manner, because healthy fathers are not sexual with their daughters.

In desperation due to unmet needs, these women turn to drugs and alcohol to numb the pain and emptiness felt by the lack of an emotional connection with a man. The sexually abused victim believes the lie that the root to intimacy is down the sexual road, when in reality the root to intimacy is down the road of self-knowledge and self-understanding and a willingness to share that with another.

Sexual damage removes from its victim a sense of self. You cannot understand something you don't realize exists. You may feel physically, but your soul is numb. Without an identity, a search for fulfillment is focused on mere external stimulation. "The tragedy of abuse," says Dr. Dan Allender, "is that the enjoyment of one's body becomes the basis of the hatred of one's soul" *(The Wounded Heart,* 85). This hatred of self makes intimacy an impossible dream. It's only when healing occurs and an identity is restored that one can find true intimacy of body and soul.

Our friend Priscilla, in her desperation to find herself, penned these words, which poetically describe the fracturing of her body and soul and her inmost longing to discover her sense of self. She calls it "Missing Person."

Where is that woman
The person I should be?
Did she wander away,
One day,
When I wasn't looking?

I think I left her,
Abandoned,
By the highway,
A long time ago.
How could I have done
Such a thing
To my best self?

Forgive me, sister—
I traded you cheaply
For a mess of pottage.
The road back is rough,
Pot-holed and neglected;
Shadows are long
In the waning light.

How smooth and sunny
It was,
When last I saw you.
Are you waiting still,
Believing in my return,
Existing on faith
In my self-loyalty?
Or, will I find,
Around that next bend,
A small and lonely
Pile of bones?
Oh, friends and lovers,
Help me find my sister!
She is too precious,
Too fragile and exquisite,
To wait alone.

Priscilla S. Perry

CHAPTER 11

God's Plan for Recovery

*"We are not responsible for what comes to us,
only for what we hold on to."*

At times you may feel the giant of rejection sitting heavily on your chest, crushing out your life and breath. Or perhaps you feel like an Eskimo fisherman who wakes after a nap to find yourself alone, floating on a small chunk of ice surrounded by a frigid sea. Are you at the place in your life where you feel that you can't hang on any longer—like the kitten clinging by its claws to the limb of a tree, hoping the rescue squad is on its way? Well, it is!

It is of utmost importance that you understand that recovery does not come by reading a book, listening to a tape, attending a lecture, or even by fervent prayer. Since the beginning of time, our enemy has been orchestrating circumstances to steal, kill, and destroy each of us (John 10:10). He actually began this process for your soul before you were born and has allowed the previous generations of your family to pass on to you their unresolved emotional pain (see Exod. 20:5, 6), thus setting you up for failure.

In the character-forming years of childhood, Satan gloated as he made sure your needs were unmet. In fact, he made sure that your parents probably were not even aware that God had placed within you the software that required that your basic needs be met in order for you to develop a character like your heavenly Father's.

You needed an *accepting father and mother* who would model healthy male and female characteristics.

You needed to be *loved unconditionally*, just because you were you. And you needed the privilege of reaching out in love to your parents in the best way you could at every stage of development and having that love accepted.

You needed to be *acknowledged*, received, heard, included, and considered important.

You needed *affirmation*, words of encouragement and praise—not just for accomplishments but for personal characteristics as well.

You needed *support*, a supply of strength and assistance to achieve.

You needed *trust* in your primary care givers—the ability to rely on them to meet your physical and emotional needs as you matured.

You needed *knowledge* and instruction equal to the level of your inquiry.

You needed *safe* and nurturing touch without fear of pain or invasion.

You needed *direction*—gentle training for decision making and the governing of self.

You needed *active participation and caring* from the significant others in your life. You needed time devoted specifically to you.

You needed a sense of *security*, a peaceful home, the pure joys of the magic of early childhood, a comfortable routine, so that life was predictable and the consistency of knowing that imposed consequences would be just—based on principles, not emotions.

And you needed *wings*. Freedom, at the appropriate age and maturity level, to make your own choices in life.

But chances are, you didn't get everything you needed. Few ever do. That's Satan's plan. He wants to imprison you in his web of dysfunction where you will be controlled by the unresolved emotional pain of your past.

But God's plan is to give you life, and to give it to you more abundantly. (See John 10:10.) Jesus says, "With Me, 'You will be free indeed'" (John 8:36). Psalm 146: 7 makes it clear: "The Lord gives freedom to the prisoners." And in Isaiah 42:7 the Lord has promised to "open eyes that are blind, and to free captives from prison and to release from the dungeon those who sit in darkness" (NIV).

When you, as a distraught prisoner, decide that you can't tolerate any more the brick walls of rejection, the steel emotional bars, or the darkness of depression that has crept into your soul, it's time to follow God's recovery plan. The escape to the light of truth and the freedom it brings takes knowledge, time, and planning. Wrong choices could lead to deeper despair.

Escape from prison involves the strategy of applying that acquired knowledge to a prisoner's past experiences of time schedules and the prison guard's habits before you dare to place your foot outside the walls that have been your false safety for so long.

Finally the day comes to implement everything you have planned—to actively take those steps that will resolve your confinement.

If you follow the plan with precision and successfully escape the walls that have kept you trapped for too long, you can breathe a sigh of relief! Why? Because your anxiety, your anger, your fears that have been a part of you in the prison of your past will be alleviated! Gone! You will be free at last!

Recovery is a process. It requires the same four steps any prisoner must take to escape confinement: acquire knowledge, apply that knowledge to yourself, actively resolve uncompleted issues, and alleviate the pain.

Acquire knowledge

First, you must learn about the prison of the mind that confines you and that determines your thoughts, feelings, and behaviors. What you have read in this book, about rejection and its effects on a life and about needs unmet and abuses endured, is essential knowledge. You must know what the human mind and body needs before you can compare what you got through personal experiences with God's ideal for you. You must also learn how parents impact the lives of their children, creating emotional immaturity and dependencies, skewing and twisting a child's view of God. What you think and feel determines how you will behave and whether your lives will be a success or failure. Christian and secular writers have produced volumes on these subjects, and the person who is serious about healing will take advantage of these resources. Four of the most helpful books we recommend are written by Dr. David A. Seamands, *Healing for Damaged Emotions, Healing of Memories, Putting Away Childish Things,* and *If Only*. Rich Buhler's book, *Pain and Pretending*, is a helpful one for discovering the causes of your codependency. *Healing the Scars of Emotional Abuse* by Gregory L. Jantz is very helpful. And if you have been sexually abused, you'll want to read *The Wounded Heart* by Dan B. Allender and fill out the workbook.

Books are not the only source of helpful information. Many ministries offer self-help audio and video tapes, seminars, or weekend retreats. In addition, just listening to Christian radio programs as they interview professionals can give you insights that you might not find elsewhere. Even the internet now offers scientific and psychological information that can help you understand yourself better. Carefully use whatever means and methods you can to increase your store of knowledge.

Apply that knowledge to yourself

As you read self-help books and take advantage of other sources of information, you must apply the knowledge you are learning to yourself personally. You must come to realize how your history has impacted who you are today and how Satan's plan to destroy and conquer God's children for his kingdom has been implemented in your own life.

Our home library is filled with self-help books and audio tapes on just about every subject you can imagine, and we have read or listened to most of them. Ron is constantly downloading late-breaking information from the internet. But the question is, Have we applied this information to our own lives?

It is easy to acquire information and pat yourself on the back for having another volume under your belt or more facts learned. But what has this information done for you? Are the books and tapes just taking up space and collecting dust or crowding some filing cabinet, or have you allowed the information to impact your life? The only way for that to happen is to read or listen as if you were on a journey and at each mile of the way you ask the question, "What have I just learned about me? How does this piece of information apply to me?"

You can be sure that the mind that tries to avoid pain will not want to acknowledge any truth that may be hurtful. And Satan, even though he cannot read your mind, can try to block you from recognizing truths that could set you free. The mind has an inborn need to honor the parent, and sometimes a misunderstanding of that honoring gets in the way of being able to see exactly what has happened to you. As long as our eyes are blinded by a misinterpretation of truth, we will be like the Laodicean church, which has need of nothing. (See Rev. 3:17.)

It may be difficult for some to comprehend that the Bible verse "The truth shall set you free" (John 8:32) can be broadened it its meaning to be more than just an understanding that Jesus wants to set us free from our sins. As pawns in Satan's kingdom, we are held captive to the thoughts and feelings that stem from childhood, and they force us into behaviors that end up being self-destructive and harmful to others.

Could it be that accepting the truth of our damage and the resulting behaviors can be the opening needed for the in-filling of the Holy Spirit? Ephesians 4:30, 31 says, "And do not grieve the Holy Spirit of God, with whom you were sealed for the day of redemption. Get rid of all bitterness, rage and anger, brawling and slander, along with every form of malice."

If it is your bitterness, rage, or anger that is keeping you from being filled with the Holy Spirit, isn't it time to get rid of it?

"Sure," you say, "but . . . I've been praying about it for years, and I still have a quick temper, and I still get angry when I think of what so and so did to me."

The secret to removing the negative emotions is to discover their origin. Early childhood is fertile ground into which seeds of bitterness, anger, and slander are sown. Each succeeding injustice done or need unmet is exaggerated by the pain felt in childhood when what we learn is absorbed through the emotions into the memory bank. Each current stimulus relates back to a previous painful childhood injury, and the current emotion is inflated by the helplessness the child felt to correct the wrong.

We must look at ourselves as in a mirror, as we see ourselves reflected there, with all our flaws in view; we must be willing to recognize our inability and Christ's sacrifice. As we humble self, we are washed in His blood, covered with His white robe of character and enabled through the Holy Spirit.

One of our tendencies is to excuse away our behaviors, saying "That's just the way I am. If you don't like it, lump it!" But wait! Jesus said you must get rid of your destructive behaviors. So where do you begin?

First, learn all you can about the damages you have received. You may ask questions of your family and friends in your search for truth about the experiences of your past. If what you learn leads you to believe that your childhood experiences were painful, then ask yourself these questions:

- How do I view myself?
- Do I have worth and value apart from what I do?
- Do I accept or reject myself?
- Do I accept or reject others?

- What behaviors do I use to keep myself from being reabused?
- Is it my tendency to deny that I have problems?
- Do I feel that I was the exception to the norm?
- Is it my tendency to feel that my family was perfect?
- Are my decisions mostly self-serving or do they consider other's needs?
- Is my tendency to put myself last while everyone else's needs get met?

Second, ask yourself if you have been able to accomplish the following emotional tasks:

- Do I trust myself and others?
- Do I have the ability to make decisions?
- Do I have initiative?
- Can I work without someone else telling me what to do?
- Do I know who I am apart from my family of origin?
- Do I have the ability to connect emotionally on an intimate level?
- Am I productive, and can I finish tasks?
- Do I have integrity? Can I look at myself in a mirror without feelings of guilt?

Once you have honestly answered these questions, you no doubt will have discovered that you are not the person you really want to be.

Third, you must determine if you really want to be healed or not. In the fifth chapter of John the story is told of the paralytic who for thirty-eight years had lain beside the pool at Bethesda. It was on a Sabbath day when Jesus passed by and noticed the scores of pathetically sick and handicapped people who were waiting for the water to ripple, erroneously thinking that if they could only be the first to enter the water, they would be healed. His heart went out to them, and He longed to touch them with His healing power, but He knew He would anger the Pharisees if He did. He continued to walk past the pool, but one man in particular caught His attention. Jesus could not ignore him. Approaching his mat, Jesus bent over and asked, "Do you want to be healed?"

Ordinarily one would consider this a foolish question. But Jesus, because He knew humanity so well, asked permission, rather than forcing His own agenda on the man. Cooperation would enhance the healing process. It is interesting to note that the paralytic did not answer Jesus' question but instead blamed his lack of support from others as the reason for his lack of healing. "Sir, I have no one to help me into the pool when the water is stirred. While I am trying to get in, someone else goes down ahead of me." Isn't that just like human nature—making excuses for our condition and then blaming others? And how does Jesus respond? He gave an order, "Get up! Pick up your mat and walk." For the man to be healed, he had to make a move. He had to make a choice and act on it! And it's the same today if you want to be healed. You can't just sit in a puddle of tears, licking your wounds; you've got to make a decision to take your first step.

Actively resolve uncompleted issues

Step 1: Commit to a lifelong process of maturing.
    We are convinced that healing from childhood damage done to us and the resulting thoughts, feelings, and behaviors is the process known as sanctification. Why would we say that? Because sanctification is the process of being set

apart for a holy purpose. And once we have begun to re-move from our lives the bitterness and malice that has clogged our communication with God; then His Spirit will flow through us to others, and our holy purpose will be to give to others the goodness and mercy of God.

Step 2: Make a list of people in your immediate family and your circle of friends and analyze that list for possible hurts. (List marital partners last.)

In the light of what you have read so far, sit with a spe-cially chosen notebook and your favorite pen or pencil or pull up a new file on your computer and ask God to help you as you go back into your memory to look at your childhood. What are you looking for?

Starting with your parents, compare their behaviors to-ward you with the list of a child's needs described earlier in this chapter. Ask yourself, Were each of these needs met to my satisfaction? Be careful not to excuse your parents be-cause a child's mind absorbs only what it sees, hears or feels, making no value judgments or excuses. Also, be careful not to blame, because most parents don't intend to inflict harm upon their children. They do so because they themselves were damaged and they don't realize the consequences of their actions. For years it has been mistakenly believed that children's feelings don't matter and that they will forget the injustices done to them. Your parents may have thought this was true.

In a recent visit with Maggie, an older woman who had suffered multiple injustices in her life and was currently living in depression, we asked the question, "Can you tell us what childhood was like for you?"

There were a few moments of silence as she stared with-out expression as if searching the halls of her memory. We knew that her family was severely dysfunctional and that she had been an abused child.

Finally deflecting her eyes down to the table in front of her and with unbelievable sadness, she replied, "My childhood ruined my whole life. I was never held. Never loved. I never felt part of the family. I remember the day I left home at age eighteen. I was packing my suitcase, and my aunt was sitting with my parents at the kitchen table. For some reason I passed through the kitchen and I heard my aunt ask my mother the question, 'Where does she think she's going? Who the hell will want her? She's such a pig.'

"I remember thinking, 'Well, nobody wants me here; they never have.' I have had three husbands, and every one of them was abusive, just like my dad. My first husband beat me all the time, and once in a while when my folks would come to visit, my father would still slug me. I guess it was just a habit. As a matter of fact, on my wedding day my father told my bridegroom that he would have to beat me once in a while to keep me in line. My mother never did like me. She never had a kind word to say or a soft touch for my bruised body. I guess she hated me because I had the same name as an old girlfriend of my father's.

"Every day," she said, "I ask God why He is keeping me alive. Why doesn't He just let me die? Then at least I could go to be with Him, the only one who has ever accepted me."

The sad thing is, we also know this woman's mother, and she has no idea why her third child has led such a dysfunctional life. It is incomprehensible to her that her daughter spent months in a state mental institution, has been in and out of three marriages, and lives a life of a recluse, taking numerous psychotropic drugs to keep emotionally stable. The mother's attitude is that you should forget the past and just live for today, as though the past had no influence on the present. But if you remember it; to you it is real. What we perceive, we receive as truth. Don't judge and evaluate yourself for telling the truth. It is that truth that has the power to set you free!

Step 3: Make a list of the damages done to you in childhood.
Here is a list of questions to ask yourself to help you determine damages inflicted on you:

- Do I feel that I am an integral part of my original family? Did I belong? Was I considered important? Did my family encourage me to do my best? Did my family care to hear my thoughts and feelings? Was home a safe place to tell the truth? Did I have a close friend in whom I could confide? Was school a safe place?

- Was I abused emotionally? In other words, Was I compared with others? Was I demeaned and made to feel inferior? Was I the victim of angry words, criticism, and loud accusations? Was I ignored? Was I laughed at or teased?

- Was I exposed to physical abuse between my parents, or parents and siblings? Was I the victim of cruel spankings or harsh unjust discipline? Did I observe cruelty to animals by other family members or friends? Did I have appropriate clothing and shoes for the weather? Was I forced to work beyond what would be acceptable by child labor laws? Was I encouraged to be the playground bully?

- Was I sexually abused in any of the following forms: (1) lack of touch, (2) observing the sexual behaviors of parents or others, (3) exposed to crude sexual language and/or behaviors before puberty, (4) touched or treated in a sexual manner, (5) exposed to nakedness of parents or older siblings and adults, (6) forced to participate in sexual behaviors, (7) exposed to pornography in any of its forms, including sexually explicit movies on television, (8) taught to masturbate myself or others.

Step 4: Make a list of those people with whom you have unfinished business.

You will know if you have unfinished business with someone if you harbor resentments, anger, bitterness, and a desire for revenge. And if your behaviors, as a result of the damage they did to you, continue to inflict pain upon you or upon others, then you will know that there is still something to be dealt with.

You may say, "Oh, I forgave them a long time ago." But forgiveness is "for giving" you peace. Do you have it? Or are the results of the damage inflicted upon you still creating chaos in your life or in someone else's life who is close to you? Forgiveness is a gift from God and is accomplished over time as we release the emotional charge contained in the memory of the injustice. The words "I forgive you" are not some magic phrase that sweeps away the past. The memory always remains. The question is, Does the memory still contain painful emotion? If so, you need to do more work in that area.

Step 5: Beginning with the most severely painful childhood memory, write a letter to all those with whom you have unfinished business.

The purpose of the letter is not for revenge or blame. It is simply to remove from you the infectious emotion that resulted from the injustice done. It is the emotional charge in your memory that flags this memory as an unhealed wound.

Why a letter? Because the hand will write what the mouth cannot say. Our fear prevents us from verbalizing our feelings. So the tendency is to sweep the pain under the rug as if it never existed. Doing this repeatedly creates a lump so large that we trip over it and suffer the results of a fall. The Bible says, "If your brother sins against you, go and show him his fault, just between the two of you" (Matt. 18:15, NIV). For most people that is a very scary thought because we fear being reabused. You will always see your perpetrator in a destructive role until you repaint the canvas.

Why would God advise us to go to others who have harmed us? It is not to shake our finger in their faces. It is not to scream accusations. It is not to destroy them but to heal ourselves. You should never hurt another in an ill-advised attempt to heal yourself. Bitterness and anger are self-destructive. The goal is not to dump your garbage in someone else's backyard but to clean up your own yard, and hopefully, theirs in the process.

Christ never accused. It's Satan who is the accuser. (See Rev. 12:10.) But we must empty ourselves, or the pain we feel will poison us and those around us.

Our job is not to excuse ourselves, but to search ourselves. We must closely examine our thoughts, feelings, and attitudes, hiding nothing from view. The blood of Christ is ours to remove the stain of sin, and the robe of His righteousness is a perfect fit! While the work of self-examination may be difficult, it *is* necessary to understand the work of pain removal we must do for the formation of Christlike character.

Here is a sample of a letter we recommend you write to those who have hurt you in some way. We have supplied the beginning of six different statements that you need to make. Complete each statement.

Dear _____,

1. The purpose of this letter is to share with you . . .

2. I want you to know that I appreciate . . .

3. I want to share with you the pain I received as a result of . . .

4. The effect on my life of the damage that was done to me has been . . .

5. My goals and plans for the future include . . .

6. This letter is being written as part of my healing process. It is to empty myself of the _____ that I have felt toward you since_____. Now that this letter is complete and I have emptied my pain, I will be filled with the Holy Spirit because that is what I have asked God to do with the void.

Now that you have looked at the basic letter, let us expand the concept or explain why each statement is important:

1. The purpose of this letter is to share with you . . .
Some possible completions comments might be ". . . my feelings about how you treated me" or ". . . the hurt I have carried since I was a child."

2. I want you to know that I appreciate . . .
Find something about the perpetrator that you can con-

sider a positive trait or behavior. No matter how abusive a person is, the person is still a child of God and has worth and value in God's sight. Their behaviors may be poor, but their worth is infinite. Don't throw out the baby with the bath water. Examples of how you might complete this statement would be, ". . . your sense of humor, your generosity, or your consistency." You might choose to give an example from your past.

3. I want to share with you the pain I received as a result of . . .

This is the section where you would recall the painful memory in detail. Describe the place, the sounds, the emotion you felt, and the details of what happened. This section may take numerous attempts to complete. In fact, that is ideal. Once you have emptied yourself of some of the pain, other feelings and sights may surface. Return to this section as many times as needed and add new insights or memories.

4. The effect on my life of the damage that was done to me has been . . .

In this section you detail how the damage has impacted every phase of your life—your relationships, your thoughts and feelings, your behaviors, your successes and failures. This, too, may take some time to complete, and returning to it several times may be necessary.

5. My goals and plans for the future include . . .

In this section you actually focus on new and improved thoughts, feelings, and behaviors, and you plan the changes you will make as a result of getting this load off your back.

6. This letter is being written as part of my healing process. It is to empty myself of the _____ that I have felt toward you since _____. Now that this letter is complete and I have emptied my pain, I will be filled with the Holy Spirit because that is what I have asked God to do with the void.

In the first blank could be written "feelings."

The second blank needs to be the main event.

The remainder of this statement is designed to help you put into words the new focus of your life. Rather than being filled with a negative emotion, you have been emptied of it and now refilled with God's Spirit.

Now what should you do with the letter? Here's what we suggest:

- Rewrite the letter so that it is no longer than two pages.

- Contact a trusted friend, counselor, or your spouse and arrange for one hour of their time. During this appointment you simply need a sympathetic ear and comforting arms. If not your spouse, choose someone of your same sex to avoid emotional complications.

- Read the letter you have rewritten out loud. You are not looking for comments or questions from your confidant, just a listening ear. As you read your eyes will see the words your hand has written, your ears will hear the words your mouth speaks, and your heart will feel the emotions that are evoked by reliving your pain. In this manner, you give to your mind messages of completion through every sense. When the painful event(s) surfaces again in the future, its powerful emotional tag will read COMPLETED.

A personal visit with the offender is ideal, where you read your letter, calmly discuss it, forgive each other, and pray together for your future. However, we live in a world of sin and abuse, and in some cases confronting the perpetrator is asking to be reabused, because of his/her control issues, defensiveness, and guilt. This is especially true for a weak victim who is just beginning recovery. It can be both frightening and risky to confront. Each situation must be evaluated carefully to determine the safest way to proceed.

If you do not know the whereabouts of your offender or if the person is dead, the letter can still be written and read aloud to a trusted party because the purpose is not for the offender but for you.

If you should choose to confront the offender personally, take with you the letter you have written and read it out loud to that person. The reason for doing this is that your fearful emotion will not get in the way of saying what needs to be said. Nor will your angry emotions distort the message.

Step 6: Accept responsibility for your thoughts, feelings and behaviors you have as a result of the damage done to you.
You are not responsible for the damage, but you are responsible for continuing to damage yourself and others—for reinfecting the wound. Ask yourself, Who have I hurt by the emotions I have harbored?

Step 7: Confess your fault to those you have damaged, asking for their forgiveness for the harm you have done to them because of your out-of-control emotions.

Step 8: Ask God to stop you short when your tendency is to think, feel, or behave as a victim or a perpetrator.
The "poor me" game is no longer appropriate for someone who has been brought back from the clasp of Satan.

Nor is need for revenge any longer your responsibility. "Vengeance is mine, I will repay, says the Lord" (Rom. 12:19, NKJV).

Alleviate the pain

This process of sanctification, once you begin it, will last a lifetime! But don't worry! It is an exciting adventure! For as you empty pain, you create space for the Holy Spirit to dwell within you as your Guide and Comforter. Then as God comes to live within you through His Spirit, He replaces your confusion with His peace. The promise is, "But the Counselor, the Holy Spirit, whom the Father will send in my name, will teach you all things and will remind you of everything I have said to you. Peace I leave with you; my peace I give you. I do not give to you as the world gives. Do not let your hearts be troubled and do not be afraid" (John 14:26, 27, NIV).

Here are some suggestions that have been helpful to us in our healing process:

- *Ask for Divine guidance.* Why? Romans 8:26 says that the Holy Spirit intercedes for us because we don't even know what we ought to pray for. And in James 4:3 we are told that we do not receive because we ask with selfish motives.

- *Be willing to forgive the offender.* Forgiveness is a divine quality, not human. The forgiveness we give to another, we must first receive from God. It is only our unwillingness, our need for revenge or rightness, that keeps us from receiving the very gift that would give us peace. Some say that if they forgive, they will be letting the perpetrator off the hook. The question is, Exactly what hook is the perpetrator on? It's you that's on the hook. You're the one saddled with the load. Your lack of forgiveness keeps you on the hook.

- *Forgive yourself for thoughts, feelings, and behaviors that have resulted from the damage done to you.* If forgiveness is a gift from God, then He can give it to you for yourself, as well as for others.

- *Think uplifting thoughts.* No, this is not New Age gobblety-goop. This is New Testament truth. Philippians 4:4-9 admonishes us to think about whatever is true, noble, right, pure, lovely, admirable, excellent, or praiseworthy. And if you do, the God of peace will be with you.

- *Memorize biblical promises.* 2 Peter 1:3,4 tells us that we become partakers of the divine nature through "exceeding great and precious promises."

- *Praise God for His renewing and regenerating power in your life.* We have discovered that one of the greatest tools to overcome negative thinking and feeling is our CD player. When the negative thoughts flood our minds, we slide in a disk, turn the volume to 9, and sing at the top of our lungs. The neighbors may wonder about our sanity, but we know we're preserving it.

Don't expect sudden miracles. But as soon as you begin the process of recovery, you will feel the emotional load you are carrying begin to lighten. Little by little, as you empty your pain, your attitude will change. One day you will realize that your conversation is more positive, your tiredness has lessened, and your future looks more promising. It is then that you will say to yourself, "I will never turn back. I will stay on this road toward recovery forever."

"There is a single path to sickness and a
thousand ways to health.
All you have to do to get worse is to keep
narrowing your horizons, your arteries, your mind,
your enthusiasms, your community, your compassion.
And to get better all you have to do is open
up to the multitudinous wonders and
healing balms within, without, and around.
Start unwinding the tangled string of your dis-ease
and knots (the nots) in your spirit will loosen."

Sam Keen,
Inward Bound:
Exploring the Geography of Your Emotions,
xi

Chapter 12

The Redeemed Shall Rejoice!

"When I was a child, I talked like a child,
I thought like a child,
I reasoned like a child.
When I became a man,
I put childish ways behind me."
1 Corinthians 13:11, NIV

Just as loving parents rejoice at the moment when a baby says "Dada" for the first time or takes those first tottering steps, we thrill at the tiniest progress made by those who have chosen to grow toward emotional maturity. Each victory, no matter how small it seems, adds courage for the next and brings excitement to those who applaud from the balcony. To those of you on the road to wholeness, it may seem that you are progressing at a snail's pace because you are anxious to get out of the pain and into the pleasure. But to those of us who watch and encourage, your every step is victory!

Scripture tells us that the Lord rejoices over you with singing (see Zeph. 3:17), and here's why. Your steady improvement toward emotional and spiritual stability declares to all those around you that God is supplying the power for your progress, that your only hope for healing comes from your connection with the Great Physician. That is cause for thunderous applause and shouts of praise because it gives hope to all of us. He is our hope, not ourselves.

The healing process does not require that you first possess a reservoir of stamina or a quarry of grit but only that you are willing to say "Lord, I can't, but You can!" As you raise your feeble hand heavenward, God the Father grabs hold of your inadequacy and fills you with enough of His ability to jump the hurdle immediately before you. With each successful jump comes increased courage to face the oncoming hurdle. The only thing you can do is to keep raising your hands heavenward in a posture of surrender, declaring "I give up, Lord! I give up on my ability and rely on yours. I give up on my control and accept Yours. I give up my stubbornness and accept instead Your stubborn love, and I give up on my knowledge and my rightness, recognizing that my need to be right prevents me from the intimate relationship that I need with You. May I accept, instead, Your wisdom and Your righteousness."

Sometimes self wants to grab the control of the healing process, saying "This is my life, and I will do this my way." It is then that you will take a step backward and find yourself reverting to the old destructive behaviors of the past. But all is not lost. You have simply taken your foot off the accelerator and placed it on the brake. And as simple as that move was, it is equally simple to find the accelerator and use it once again. Christ does not move away because you have released your hold on Him but rather waits silently and patiently until you recognize that you have lost the power to make progress. As soon as you are aware of your mistake, you can simply make the minor adjustment toward the power pedal. And the more you practice driving with God as the power, the easier it is to keep attached to the source of power for the entire length of your journey.

It's encouraging to hear of the progress of others on the road to recovery as their successes help us to realize what is possible for ourselves. Because that is so, let's revisit some of those whose stories have been revealed in this book and see what God is doing in the lives of His redeemed today.

The story of Jenny's ritualistic satanic abuse at the hand of her father and others (see chapter 2), has created shivers in most who have heard it. However, nothing is too hard for the Lord. (See Mark 10:27.) Jenny has made significant changes as she has held onto the hand of God for her healing. Not only did Jenny choose to process through her own healing, but as she progressed and noticed the physical and emotional changes that healing brings, she received the courage to grow in other ways. Jenny returned to school and completed the college degree she had started many long years ago. Subsequently, she went on to graduate school and completed a degree in journalism. We hope that some day soon Jenny will write her complete story of what God has done for her.

She and her physician husband have found a new depth of intimacy in their marriage, which they had thought was impossible. Together they enjoy their grandchildren and a fulfilling social life. They are actively involved in their church and in their community.

But more than this, it's the sparkle in Jenny's eyes and her new zest for living that convinces us that as difficult as our work is at times, it's well worth it. The last time we passed through the town where Jenny and Burt live, we called to touch base. Burt answered the phone and within seconds had made arrangements for us to have dinner at their home. Jenny raced to the door and with the enthusiasm of a child hugged and danced around her old friends. Dinner was creatively prepared and a delight to the palate. When the meal was over, Jenny unashamedly excused the men, sending them to the living room so she and I (Nancy) could talk. "Nance, I've got a box full of stuff I want to show you. It's pictures of me when I was a child, old newspaper clippings, a doll that I had way back then, and a few other things. You want to see?"

The little girl Satan tried to trap in his web with the most gross abuse that one can imagine, God had released and, indeed, made her free!

Kristy, whose story is told in chapter 10, was a hurting but physically beautiful woman in her late thirties when we first met. Her very concerned mother brought her to me (Nancy) for some assistance to sort out the complexities of her current life. At first glance, I saw a well-groomed business woman who appeared to be in perfect control of her life, but after moments in the counseling office, it became apparent that she had learned well to cover her fears with a façade of professionalism.

She seemed comfortable to concentrate on the overwhelming circumstances of her current situation, but when I asked her to share with me the events of her childhood, she became stone-faced and obviously fearful of that exposure. She was, however, quick to tell me that her memories of childhood were vague and filled with pain. As her story unfolded, her anxiety increased. "I really don't want to talk about this," she said. "Do we have to? What has the past got to do with my current problems?"

"Kristy, what happened early in childhood always influences what is happening today. The past may be painful to look at, but it has set up the thought, feelings, and behaviors you have now. We don't have to look at it all today. But you need to know that in order to be healed, you must confront those skeletons in your emotional memory closet and remove from them the power to frighten and control you now. Healing is a process that takes time, and little by little as memories surface, I will help you to be able to work through them, removing the debilitating emotion they contain. As we do this together, you will discover that your present circumstances will be easier to manage and healthy decisions will come to you more naturally. But you have to make the choice to proceed or to leave things as they are," I counseled.

I cannot testify that Kristy's road to recovery was without potholes and frightening curves, yet her willingness to stay on the path paid off in the end. As she neared the end of her counseling sessions with me, she entered the office for one appointment with a whole new demeanor and atmosphere about her. She could hardly wait for the usual opening prayer before blurting out a victory that had occurred just that day. "I did it! I did it! I did it!" she exclaimed with joyous abandon.

"What, Kristy? What did you do?"

"At the office today a fellow I had seen in passing came to my desk. He opened with casual conversation, then he invited me to dinner. But before I could give him my answer, he made a sexual proposition about his after dinner plans. I got right up in his face! Honestly, Nancy, I can't believe I did this, but I pointed my finger right at his nose and emphatically asked, 'Just what kind of a woman do you think I am? You're barking up the wrong tree. If you want sex, you'll have to get it somewhere else!' "

What a victory! I rejoiced with her that God had given her the power to say the words that she wished for a lifetime she could have said to her father, but could not.

She continued, "And now, Nancy, I feel so free! It's like being on a motorcycle with the wind blowing through your hair. I didn't know this was possible. Thank you. Thank you."

(Nancy and Ron) Then there was Vicky. Her story is found in chapter 10. She was the one who not only was a victim of incest and physical abuse but was married to an incest victim as well. Remember, Vicky and Dave's honeymoon began in twin beds because of Dave's fear of intimacy.

The process of their recovery began six years ago and continues today. One thing we must understand is that recovery once begun never ends. Little by little God reveals to us pieces of our past that will assist us to experience joy in our present. Spiritually, it's sanctification—the process of being made holy.

Not long ago we were talking to someone who mentioned this couple and said, "There is no more dramatic and beautiful example of lives changed than Vicky and Dave. Even if you ignore the behavioral changes, you can't overlook the countenance changes. This couple looks so vibrant, so alive, so healthy, so happy. And since the process of recovery began, they have survived more traumas than most couples encounter in their lifetimes. They have held hands and laid back in the Lord's arms, laughed about it, cried about it, and allowed their misery to bring them even closer together."

At one time or another almost all have felt like victims; resentful of people whom we feel have been unfair or downright intentionally destructive and cruel. For years, I (Nancy) resented my father. I resented his rulership in my life, the caustic and demeaning words he said to me. On the other hand, I admired his talent and wisdom. My father was a good man who himself carried the pain of rejection from his original family. One who is filled with pain cannot give out pleasure to others—especially to his own child—for it had never been modeled to him in his own childhood. What he received is what I got. For years, even long after his death, I hid my resentment well. Perhaps you could say I was confused. How do admiration and lack of respect for the same person coexist peacefully in one's mind?

My husband ended up paying the price because I expected him to do all of the things for me that my father did not do and be all the things to me my father was not. Whenever there is lack in a parental figure, the spouse is expected to fill that emptiness, and that's an impossibility. It was not until I actually jumped into recovery with both feet that I began to learn some things that could have saved both Ron and me much heartache had we known when we first married.

I had spent forty years looking at my dad through the eyes of a child. The child said, "Daddy, play with me. Fix my hurt. Love and adore me. Take care of my needs. Bring home little gifts and surprises that would tickle my fancy. Don't scold and reprimand me. Just love me, adore me, and accept me."

When I married, I expected that my husband ("Daddy Ron") would do all those things for me, but he carried his own sense of mother-emptiness and expected me to fill all of his mother needs. We were two adults behaving like two little children. What a miserable pair!

The process of recovery is about emptying the painful emotion connected to our memories. As the pain leaves us, we begin to look at our parents through different eyes—adult eyes. The adult says, "Mommy and Daddy are no longer responsible to fill my needs. I cannot look to them to alleviate my hurt, to make me feel good about who I am, to solve all my problems and grant all my wishes." Why not, because Mommy and Daddy had their own issues. They were frail; they were hurting; they had been damaged, and so it has been since Adam and Eve.

In order to heal, my perspective had to change. Yet it didn't happen without a struggle. Instead, I used the "yea but" method of reasoning: "Yea but, if my father had not been absent during my first four years because of the war, I could have bonded with him." "Yea but, if my daddy had just been more patient and tolerant with me, I could have probably been the pianist he dreamed I would be." "Yea but, if he had only said those three words I longed to hear and affirmed the good things I did, I wouldn't have looked to everyone else longing to hear "I love you" or "You did good."

So what do we do? Spend our lives saying "if only," playing the blame game, and sitting in muck, never able to move on to feelings of success and acceptance? Absolutely not!

First, we rid ourselves of the hurtful emotion. (See chapter 11.) And then we say to ourselves, "Your parents were only human after all, and they did the very best they could with what they had. Finally, as we mature spiritually, we begin to see our parents through the eyes of God who says, "Regardless of your behavior, I love you." He is able to separate worth and value from behavior. And we must too. Of course, God does not tolerate or overlook sin, but He does understand it and calls us to greater excellence.

Recovery is a process. It doesn't happen overnight because we've read one book or attended a weekend intensive recovery seminar. And this has been true in my case. Here's my latest chapter in the story of my recovery from rejection:

Not long ago, Ron and I took our friends for an afternoon drive. I had brought along a case of cassette tapes so we could enjoy some Sabbath music. I opened the case, looked through the tapes, and saw two tapes entitled "James Hallas." I pulled one from the case and handed it to Ron in the front seat, saying, "Why don't you put this in the tape deck." Ron did so without looking at the title. I sat back in my seat and as I heard the beautiful hymns played in my father's own inimitable style, my tears began to flow. No one else in my family knew I had these tapes. But Ron knew immediately who was playing the piano and turned his head with a knowing smile.

My friend, Donna, said to me, "Whose tape is that? Is that Dino?" When I turned my head toward her to answer, she saw the tears and exclaimed, "Oh, my God. It's your dad. How could I forget? It's your dad." The tears flowed for quite some time before I could speak a word.

Donna had reached over and grabbed my hand because she knew I was hurting. Finally I said to her, "You know, that's the first time I've listened to that tape without feeling the knots of resentment inside me. It's the first time I really remember, in all these years since my father has been gone, missing him. There have been a flood of good memories while I have listened to this tape just now, and I have another tape of Daddy. Do you mind if we listen?"

Believe it or not, it felt good to let the tears flow, to see Daddy's face, to see him sitting at the piano and to feel the loss. Sometimes it takes a long time to grow up. I've learned the hard way. But you don't have to wait a lifetime to heal. You can take the steps to recovery now.

Why did the last stronghold of my resentment give way when it did? I was in another process of recovery at the time—recovery from knee surgery. Ron and I were in the car with dear friends with whom I felt safe, and the ride was just to get me out of the house to divert my attention from the pain. My house had indeed become a house of mourning as I found myself crying uncontrolably from the unrelenting physical pain from which I was suffering. I was emotionally raw. My defenses were down—I had no psychological energy to resist. And I think God uses times like these to teach us lessons we might not be open to in better times. The wisest man who ever lived made this comment: "It is better to go to a house of mourning than to go to the house of feasting. . . . Sorrow is better than laughter, because a sad face is good for the heart (mind). . . . For there is a proper time and procedure for every matter, though a man's misery weighs heavily upon him" (Eccles. 7:2, 3, 6, NIV; parentheses added).

When I had read these verses previously, they didn't make sense. I had always believed the proverb "A merry heart does good, like medicine, But a broken spirit dries the bones" (Prov. 17:22, NKJV). Since I knew a broken spirit depressed the immune system, how could times of sorrow be good for the heart? Suddenly these verses had meaning to me. God had used my time of physical pain to relieve my emotional pain. Interesting, isn't it? And indeed, my heart—or more accurately, my mind, was better for it.

These recovery stories are heartwarming. But you may be saying, "Of course, there's hope if you're a victim, but what about abusers? Haven't you heard the statement, 'Once an abuser; always an abuser?' Is it possible for a leopard to really change his spots? What if I'm an abuser, is there hope for me?"

One has to remember that abusers don't just wake up one morning during childhood or their teen years and say,

"I think I will spend my life being a criminal, hurting people, taking lives, and punishing my family and those I care about." That's someone else's agenda. Remember? Satan is a user. And he uses damaged boys and girls and creates out of them damaging adults.

Is God not powerful enough to thwart Satan's purpose? We believe He is. And here's why:

On a tiny U.S. territorial island in the vast South Pacific, generational war still rages. Domestic violence is rampant; drugs flow freely, and abuse is no respecter of persons or positions. From the jungle huts to the palatial condos, emotional and spiritual pain abounds. It was here that we were called by a Christian mission clinic to hold a series of meetings, hoping to educate professionals and community members by helping them learn how to recover from the relational curse that has escalated since the 1500s when all the male population was slaughtered and the women impregnated by men from another culture. We have been there three times and have held numerous seminars for government, educational departments, social services, mental health, the judicial system, the shelter system, and several churches.

On our second visit we held a spiritual recovery seminar called "Binding the Wounds" for a large church congregation. We had no idea that in our audience were two men who had been sent by the department of mental health because of drug addiction and domestic violence. They were currently in a lock-up unit for drug rehab, and amazingly, they were ordered to attend the fourteen-hour seminar. Their wives were encouraged to meet them there. We gave a number of other seminars on the island, including one at the Hyatt Regency Hotel, but it wasn't until a year later that we learned the impact our ministry had on the lives of these two men—and one other. Here's what happened:

One year later we returned to the island for three more weeks of meetings. On our first evening, we opened a marriage weekend designed to teach couples in-depth communication skills. In our opening exercise we asked that each person give their name, where they lived, how they heard about the seminar, and what they hoped to gain from it. The first gentleman who spoke stood to his feet and said, "My name is David. One year ago I was addicted to crack cocaine, smoked four packs of cigarettes a day, was an alcoholic, was married to my third wife, whom I regularly abused both physically and emotionally, and had about fifteen other lovers on the side. My wife and I attended the seminar you taught at the Hyatt Regency last year. I was hoping you would be able to fix her. Today, I want you to know that I am the one who has been fixed. I no longer take drugs. I no longer smoke cigarettes. I no longer drink alcohol, I no longer beat my wife, and I am faithful to her alone.

"During your seminar you suggested that we investigate our own family history to discover what generational pain we may be carrying. My family has lived for generations on this island, but I knew very little about them because almost all of my older relatives were deceased. A friend suggested that I go to the university, which has records of many of the old island families. I did this, and to my utter amazement, I discovered that my grandfather had beheaded my grandmother with a machete. I thought back to my own childhood, and I remembered the fear, the anger, and the sadness of growing up in a very violent family. I thought to myself, *Here I am carrying on the family tradition of violence and for what? Am I happy? What am I doing to my children? How I must be damaging my poor little wife, Bertha!"*

"I made up my mind then and there. 'This garbage stops with me.' My wife and I joined the recovery program we had learned about at your seminar. And the changes in our lives have been dramatic."

Bertha sat beside him nodding her head in agreement, and we were speechless. Directly across from us was a physician and his wife who had facilitated the recovery classes David had attended. Glancing over at them, we noticed that they were both crying too. How could we not?

There was hardly a moment to gain composure when Bob, an American who had lived on the island for twenty years, stood to his feet. "One year ago, Robby (he pointed to a fellow across the circle) and I were in a lock-up unit for drug rehabilitation. I was a wife batterer, a druggie, an alcoholic, and so sexually addicted that I would leave my wife home alone and go to the bars where I drank and had sex with several women an evening.

"Both Robby and I attended the meetings you held at the church because our mental health worker ordered us to do so. What I learned so changed my life that I wondered what else this church might have to offer that could benefit me. I noticed a sign for some evangelistic meetings beginning in a few days, and Robby and I came up with a plan to manipulate our way out of the lock-up unit to attend them. Today I am a baptized Christian, the head deacon of that church, and the founder of four Narcotics Anonymous groups that meet at the church twice a week. Between thirty to fifty people attend each session. I volunteer at the Christian radio station, and any other spare time I have, I donate to the church or the recovery program."

Then it was Robby's turn. "I don't know how to start," he

said, "and I'm very emotional so I probably will cry. Bob is right. But what he doesn't know about that night when we first went to the seminar is that I was plotting my suicide by jumping off Lovers' Leap (a 400-foot cliff where many have jumped to their death). I, too, was addicted like both of these men. My wife who sits beside me tonight is my fourth. At the time of the Vietnam War, I joined the Marines and was trained as an assassin. It was my job to enter villages at night and slit the throats of the enemy. I did my job well. The last assignment I received was to murder the Vietnamese woman I loved and with whom I had borne two children. I was ordered to murder them also. I had no idea that they were Vietcong."

With his head in his hands he began to sob. Through his tears he shared how each day and each night was a nightmare. "I am a Christian now, but how can I get rid of these memories and the guilt? How can I ever be forgiven for what I've done? It has always seemed that my only choice was to either numb the pain with drugs or alcohol or to end my life.

"After I attended your seminar, I had hope for the first time. But the memories of the atrocities I have committed still haunt me. I give them to God, and it seems to go well for a few hours or days, and then they are back. It's not easy to just shut off your old life and start a new one in three days. Just a week ago, I became so desperate that suicide again became a welcome out. I began again to plan my demise. I thought to myself, *You'll never see Ron Rockey again. Why would he ever want to come back to a place like this, and if he did, what would be my chances of seeing him?* And then Bob called me and said that you folks were back and that my wife and I could attend this seminar. I still have a hard time believing that after all I have done, God could possibly love me."

At this point, I (Ron) got up from my seat, knelt in front of Robby and asked, "What could you have done to be so bad that God could not forgive you?"

"All those people I killed and the wives I have beaten; the drugs, the alcohol, the sex. How can I undo it?"

"You can't undo it. But, Robby, God loves you regardless of your behavior. He separates your behavior from your worth and value and sees your value as infinite."

"But if you only knew the stuff that goes on in my head," Robby countered.

"I do know the stuff that goes on in your head; and so does God. Let me tell you about it."

And at this point I shared with Robby what for years had haunted me; what I knew was creating within him the hopelessness and the fear of eternal punishment. I reminded him of King David, of his multiple sins, and yet God called him "a man after His own heart."

When Robby didn't seem to respond, I shouted in frustration, "And I love you, Robby. Don't you get it? If I can love you when I don't even know you, why would you think God, who created you, wouldn't love you?" At that point, Robby put his head on my shoulder, and we held each other, and the tears flowed freely—both ours and all who witnessed.

We spent more time together during the next two weeks, and just before leaving the island, we all met at a local radio station that had given us permission to use their equipment to make a recording. David, Bob, and Robby each shared their stories and told about the dramatic changes

God had made in their lives. Robby ended with "If God can change my sick head, he can change anyone."

The three men have now linked arms and purposes, determined that their island nation will be turned around by God's grace. They are willingly putting time, effort, and money into supporting and assisting in the recovery of others whose stories are similar to their own.

If you are an abuser and have similar doubts as Robby had, let me assure you, God loves you. I, too, was an abuser, and God has become the loving daddy that I never had and has taken my inabilities and given me His abilities.

Since we have told the successful recovery stories of others, perhaps I (Ron) should now tell my own. In each seminar I teach, whether it be exclusively to men or to a mixed audience, I speak of the depths of my pain and the resulting dysfunctional behaviors that controlled me for so many years. I sit before others unashamedly telling the truth and sharing the path I needed to take to break out of the prison of my past.

Many have asked, "How can you do it? How can you sit there and bare your soul to people who could easily spread rumors that your past is still who you are today, and thus tarnish your ministry? You are so transparent." And they're right. I am transparent. But what I have found is that the truth about myself sets me free. As I confess it publicly, I force myself to be accountable, and the power of God is there to help me do so.

If my truth can cause someone in deep pain to listen and to receive the help they need to get out of their entrapment, then I feel God calls me to be open and tell the truth. Am I ashamed of the old life? Of course! Do I understand why I was so driven? Yes, thank God, I do understand. And now I continue to be driven to proclaim the power in God's Word to change my shameful behavior and make something beautiful out of my life.

God takes us in stages in our recovery. He gives us what we need when He knows we need it. One of the latest chapters in my recovery happened at a small seminar designed for married couples that Nancy and I were teaching. It was there that God gave me a message I could not ignore. We were in a tiny chapel in the woods. One whole wall of the chapel was wood, and beautifully carved into it were the words, "Holy, Holy, Holy, Lord God Almighty." The wall was to my right and while its color was dark, there seemed to be a piercing light annoying my right eye, and the words "Holy, Holy, Holy" kept repeating themselves in my head. I tried to ignore the irritation and kept teaching.

As the annoyance turned to pain, I recall rubbing my eye and thinking, "Something must be wrong with my eye." All Friday evening and for most of the next day the irritation continued until I finally, in my head, said to God, "What do you want, God? Holy what?"

And the answer came back, "Holy, Holy, Holy," over and over again. Finally by Saturday night it came to me that God was asking me to give up the lie at the core of my being, which told me that I had no worth and value. I had to give up my rejection that was standing between me and the holiness of God Almighty.

I said "No way, God. If I give that up, who am I?"

But God was relentless. He would not let me go.

Finally having become very familiar with confession, I blurted out right in the middle of the seminar, "If I only had a three-pound mallet and an overgrown spike about a foot long, I would take care of my rejection forever." And that, I thought was the end of it. I had made an impossible condition for getting rid of the rejection.

The next morning we returned for the final day of the seminar. I took my usual seat and was just about ready to begin when in walked one of the seminar participants holding up some things in his hands, saying, "Is this what you wanted, Ron?" As he came closer, I recognized a large mallet and a foot-long spike.

I was startled! I said "Thank you," but inside I said "No way!" I was still fighting God.

During our final break just before the seminar ended, I gave up. I took a piece of paper from my notebook and wrote with a marker pen in large letters, "MY REJEC-TION!" and said to Nancy, "I'm going to nail it, do you want to come?"

The two of us, who had been through so much pain and anguish together, walked up a fern-covered path until I spotted a huge tree stump. I laid the paper down on the stump, put the spike in the center of the paper, and with the mallet I began to drive the spike through the paper into the stump. But God wasn't done with me yet. As the spike went into the stump, it took the paper with it, and the paper with my rejection on it became injected into the stump. Weeping, Nancy and I stood there looking at the spike's head flattened against the stump with only a narrow ruffle of paper surrounding it. My sin was nailed to the tree. The miracle is that the spike, which can easily go right through ordinary paper, did not. Symbolically, it was as if God was saying "I don't want you to look at your rejection again. It is buried in the wood of the cross."

My last hold out was gone. I had used my rejection as the crutch on which I leaned. It was the excuse I gave myself and others for all of my worthless feelings and behaviors. Christ had paid the price, and that day I met Him at the cross and crucified what was left between Him and me. And now I can sing with new meaning, "Holy, Holy, Holy," for God truly is Almighty.

(Ron and Nancy) As we look back on our lives, we both realize that from the moment we were formed in our mother's wombs, God had a plan for us. It is sometimes so overwhelming to us that He would take two individuals from entirely different backgrounds, from different parts of the country, with opposite values and life perspectives, and bring them together in the miraculous way He did with us. After all, how many people meet in a courtroom?

While our first twelve years together were tortuous to us both, looking back from our perspective now, we would not change a thing. Oh yes, it would have been wonderful if our marriage had been perfect from the start and we had been perfect parents, raising perfect children, but that's a dream world. God has carried us through many a valley and lifted us over many a mountain. And each experience was for a purpose. Had we not had these experiences, it would be most difficult to comprehend the feelings and heartaches of others in similar circumstances. Now we can say "We've been there, done that, and God never abandoned us. We have learned that we are rejected no more!

That's why Isaiah 43:1-5 (NIV) means so much to us. Before sharing this passage with you, however, let us explain the meanings behind two words.

Waters: literally urine. The waste you have made of your own life.

Rivers: Troubles

Now with this understanding, let God speak to you in His words:

> *But now, this is what the Lord says—*
> *he who created you, O Jacob,*
> *he who formed you, O Israel:*
> *"Fear not, for I have redeemed you;*
> *I have summoned you by name;*
> *you are mine.*
> *When you pass through the waters,*
> *I will be with you;*
> *and when you pass through the rivers,*
> *they will not sweep over you.*
> *When you walk through the fire,*
> *you will not be burned;*
> *the flames will not set you ablaze.*
> *For I am the Lord, your God,*
> *the Holy one of Israel, your Savior; . . .*
> *Since you are precious and honored in my sight,*
> *and because I love you,*
> *I will give men in exchange for you,*

and people in exchange for your life.
Do not be afraid, for I am with you . . .

You can now rejoice with us, for we are all redeemed and rejected no more!